Coaching Hacks: Simple Strategies to Make Every Conversation More Effective
By Jonathan Reitz, MCC

Coaching Hacks: Simple Strategies to Make Every Conversation More Effective

Some of this material appeared originally on www.jonathanreitz.com.

Feel free to quote with attribution in any work. For additional training on the Coaching Hacks, please contact jonathan@jonathanreitz.com.

Published by CoachNet Global in association with Three Clicks Publishing
Copyright© 2017

Coaching Hacks: Simple Strategies to Make Every Conversation More Effective
ISBN 978-164136372-3

Printed in the United States of America

12-132017 1

Dedication

To coaches everywhere...you ask the questions that hack the world.

To Joyce...you said "Yes!" to the most important question I've ever asked!

To Julia...you taught me about being a dad and what a family is all about.

To Judy Pence and the CoachNet team...thanks for journeying with me as we hacked each other's coaching and figured out how to help coaches of all stripes and kinds...

To Mike Perkinson, Bob Sitze, Jim Martin, Dave Ambrose, Tom McMillen, Dominic Rivkin, Austin Ryan, Craig Bigby and Jason Barnhart...I wouldn't be who I am today without you men.

Prologue

#coachinghacks

Hacks are simple ideas designed to make life easier. They might save you *time* or *money* or *both*. The core of a hack is that it's an alternative way to get something done more quickly than the traditional route. And it can be *ANYTHING*.

always?

Hmmm...this sounds a lot like coaching.

My chosen profession, leadership or executive coaching, is designed to help leaders, managers, and people with influence make a bigger difference in a shorter period. You might think of coaching as a way to accelerate your impact...and this book is designed to help you hack every single conversation, coaching or other.

only purpose

The following isn't the same kind of hack:

a hack

A person who is a professional at some service, but does crappy work.
                    http://www.urbandictionary.com/define.php?term=hack

Hacking is 'an appropriate application of ingenuity.' Whether the result is a quick-and-dirty patchwork job or a carefully crafted work of art, you have to admire the cleverness that went into it.
                    http://www.catb.org/jargon/html/meaning-of-hack.html

If you're wondering how other people are using Coaching Hacks, please follow the hashtag #coachinghacks on Twitter, Facebook and Instagram. You'll find plenty of inspiration in our feeds!

About Jonathan Reitz

Jonathan Reitz, MCC is an executive and leadership coach who works with leaders to develop more clarity on who they are and where they are going, design useful action plans, and get more done in less time. He lives in Medina, Ohio with his wife Joyce and 15-year-old daughter Julia.

About CoachNet

CoachNet has been training, developing and supporting excellent coaches since 1999. CoachNet's Integrated Coach Training is available online and can cover up to 150 hours of coach specific training (coachnet.org/training).

Table of Contents

Coaching Hacks: Simple Strategies to Make Every Conversation More Effective

Introduction

It's been more than 20 years, 4,000 coaching hours, 500+ clients, and all kinds of changes (both in me and the people I've coached) since I discovered coaching. Or, more accurately, since coaching discovered me.

I love to coach. I do. When a coaching conversation is going well, the world is at your client's feet. There's nothing better.

Coaching is powerful. At the risk of raving, coaching just makes everything better. I believe coaching can do anything. Really. Anything.

Maybe a clearer way to say this would be to say a person being coached can do anything. And I think you, the reader, want to explore how to make things possible for other people. (You wouldn't be reading this book if you weren't interested in what coaching can do.)

Let's make a critical distinction as we get started: there is a difference between coaching--which we describe as using specific skills to develop or benefit another person--and being a coach, which only happens when those skills become so integrated that they inform your worldview and influence every single conversation you have.

Over the course of these pages, you will learn to do the things coaches do to make your conversations more effective. Call it using coaching hacks. Or, if you're a coach, these simple steps, or hacks, will make you more effective. But I'm going to guess that the things we're going to talk about are NOT what you're expecting.

Right now, in your head, you've probably got an image of the coach of a sports team. A mad genius, pacing up and down the sidelines of the team's game. Maybe screaming at the officials, and occasionally melting down on one of the players.

You can see that coach, just on the edge of fury, can't you?

At the core of this mental picture is a man--because it's a man you have been picturing, right?--who's doing everything in his power to get the best out of the players on his team. I think that commitment to getting the best out of the people around you is powerful.

But there's a different kind of coach that is quietly taking her place at the center of people development processes. She's not a mad genius, there's no pacing up and down the sideline, and certainly no meltdowns.

The only similarity between the two types is a deep commitment to getting the best out of the people being coached.

But what is this kind of coaching? Simply put...it's a conversation that takes someone to a place they've never been before, and challenges them to do something new when they get there.

How does that sound? Is that something you would be open to? Cool. Then, let's get at it by asking some questions that start with "What?" That's a very coach-like thing to do.

Question #1: What is a coach?

Try this simple definition: *A coach is someone who chooses to invest what they've been given to accelerate someone else's development or accomplishment.*

You might offer your experience, your skills, your time, your money...it could be anything. There are plenty of places where the broad term "coach" is the right one.

There are lots of kinds of coaches...but the common thread that runs through coaches is a desire to see other people live into their potential and accomplish what is most important to them. **We do this by making a simple mindset shift, from searching for the right answer to searching for the right question.**

Being a coach means you are helping someone else do what they feel called to accomplish. You're not doing the work for them; you're greasing the wheels so they can get to their vision.

Coaches have a particular, integrated skill set that helps them use their experience to listen deeply and ask the best questions they can. It's not about statements or directions. Coaches explore with the people they coach (whom we'll call clients). Over time, coaches draw action steps and meaningful commitments out of the people with whom they work.

When a client engages a coach, things happen. Results get achieved. The client learns about themselves and the world around them. Things change. It's powerful. Coaches make things happen.

And I think you can do it because my story is an example.

My Story

Lots changed for me when I started focusing on asking the right question instead of finding the right answer.

My first career was in radio and television, and in April 1997, I ended up on a team challenged with coming up with some new shows that my tv station could produce locally. Sort of a "going-back-to-our-roots" thing.

The three-day meeting was booked at a downtown hotel. On the first morning, Steve, a guy our general manager brought in, began working with us to brainstorm ideas. He asked a few simple questions, and before long, we had a list we were going to explore.

About 45 minutes in, I thought "This guy is helping us see what's possible."

The hook was set. The person next to me absently nodded a few minutes later when I said: "I don't know what that guy is doing, but that's what I'm supposed to do with my life."

Maybe you can relate to what was running through my mind.
- "He's focused on us."
- "We're making progress on this because of him."
- "We don't know where we're going, but he seems to know how we're going to get there."
- "No idea is a bad idea in this conversation, but we're not going to act on every idea."
- "We are picking the action steps we want to take."

Admittedly, the work my team was doing fell out of my head. The way this guy accelerated our progress was amazing, and I couldn't focus on anything other than *"how is he doing it?"*

At the break, I asked him. He told me he was a coach. I wondered if he knew where we were going to end up. He said no, and added that he DID know how to structure the conversation, so we figured out on our own where to land.

Pretty soon I was asking "How can I learn to be a coach?" Seeing Steve coach, just for a short time, made me re-think how I was spending my life. I had new possibilities. (See *Coaching Changes Everything!*)

After the break, Steve put us back to work. The way he listened to every single comment our team made added clarity to what we were doing. Follow up questions focused the conversation. He carefully drew out our opinions, and when the time was right, he invited us to make some decisions and take action. He found what was most important to us and helped it become real.

I didn't know it at the time, but we'd see Steve several more times over the next few months as we launched some new TV shows. Every time it was generous listening to understand what our team was saying, bold questions that nudged us forward and drawing out action steps to help us chart a course.

Thinking back to those first few sessions, a statement I now make all the time frames the work Steve did: Coaching is a conversation with a focus leading to a relationship with a purpose.

My coach training began a little later, and what seemed so comfortable watching Steve, I learned is pretty difficult. Coaching skills, in fact, take about a minute to learn–*seriously!*–but can take a lifetime to master.

My first challenge was learning that coaching was not about me, but rather it's about the client. As a coach, you don't direct the conversation or offer your opinion. That's what consultants do. Coaches are much more generous than that. Coaches build an other-oriented space for the client to discover what's most important to them

My friend Dominic is a great example. He is a pastor who was asking hard questions about his calling and his congregation when he hired me to coach him. To be honest, I thought his church was thriving when we started. I wanted to encourage him, pump him up and tell him his church would be enormous before too long.

But that would have been directing the conversation, not being a coach.

As we talked, Dominic kept saying that he wanted to work with multiple churches and organizations, as partners not as members. He loved his church but kept feeling that he'd be a better service to God's kingdom if he were in some other situation. But he couldn't find it.

To be honest, I just wanted to tell him *"YOUR CHURCH IS GROWING! What do you mean your calling is somewhere else? If I were you, I wouldn't be thinking about going anywhere; I'd be thinking about how I could get better at leading this church!"* But fortunately, I bit my tongue. And didn't direct the conversation. It was hard, but improving his leadership skills was not what Dominic wanted to pursue.

One question that always comes up in training is "If I'm not directing the conversation, how will I know what to talk about?" It's easy. Your client will tell you.

What? It's true. Surrendering the agenda was the second big challenge I faced when learning to coach. The client always gets to choose. Not sometimes. Not occasionally. Always. (I still struggle with this from time-to-time.)

Not only does the client choose the topic, but also how deep a conversation goes. The deeper the conversation, the more possibility for lasting change. But the client gets to choose. A masterful coach allows her clients to work on the presenting symptoms, or dive deep to the causes.

It's been 20+ years since my first encounter with that coach named Steve and the beginning of my coaching career. But the total lack of control a coach has in coaching conversation still amazes me: You can't coach what your client won't say.

Here's something I wish I'd learned sooner: Lots of good things can come from being about my growth, but it's much better to focus on someone else's growth first and mine second.

All day every day, that's what I get to do as a coach. And it's pretty spectacular.

By the way, Dominic went out and started a new ministry organization called LINC in Los Angeles, working to connect local leaders to impact their neighborhoods. Check them out at www.lincla.org. It's what he's called to do.

And just like how a coach helped me find my calling, I now get to help others find their calling. I'm a coach. And that's one of the things that coaches do.

Question #2: What is Coaching?

Coaches are people (at least most of us). Coaching is what we do. But don't stop there. Coaching is also HOW WE do what we do. It's a skill set, a mindset, and a lifestyle.

At surface level, coaching is the power to help people learn about themselves, get unstuck and get moving forward toward what they want. But it's *more than that...*

Let me challenge you to think about coaching as a mindset that makes things possible for other people. What things? Virtually ANY thing.

You get to pick. Coaching can help you start a business. Deepen your faith. Test out some new ideas or practices. Parent your kids. Patent a new product. Close a chapter in your life. If you can name it (or get someone else to name it, assuming you're the coach), a solid coaching relationship and process can help.

When I'm in my coaching mindset, I see possibilities that I don't see otherwise. So do my clients. **When you dig under the surface, coaching becomes a relational way to grow, make sense of the world and solve problems.**

The coaching mindset is both vigorous and valuable. I can charge for it. I can use it to make a living, or sometimes, I can give it as a gift.

Coaching is a lifestyle. It touches everything. It's like listening to music...always there, capable of adding a lot of beauty, meaning and experience to your life, but you're not always even aware of it.

Coaching is a way of life. It slips into the cracks of your relationships. Before you know it, you're coaching all the time. **Coaching is a way of giving structure to the relationships you have in the world.**

Coaching builds on how you think about yourself, the people you connect with, the problems you face and how you manage it all.

So, the question facing you right now is: do you have something you need help to happen (do you need a coach)? Or do you want to help make someone else's dream come to life (do you want to become a coach)?

I bet you do. And you're ready for coaching.

Question #3: What is a Hack?

Put the term "hack" into google. Type out "What is a hack?" Go ahead. I'll wait.

I've done this 10-15 times while working on this book. Here are a few of my favorite responses:

- an innovative way to accomplish a familiar task.
- A shortcut.
- Typically it would be a new way to do an old thing.
- 'an appropriate application of ingenuity'
  (http://www.catb.org/jargon/html/meaning-of-hack.html)

You'll also find references to practical jokes, bad journalists, and cyber attacks. One common thread runs through them all: A hack takes the conventional wisdom, the typical, expected way of doing things, and turns it on its ear.

Most hacks are time-efficient. They're short cuts or a quick path to a result you want. They're often non-traditional and sometimes unexpected. That's why when someone unexpected lets themselves into a computer system or a website, it's called a hack.

I'd suggest to you that coaching, at a masterful level, does the same thing. A coaching relationship is a fast, effective way to turn a client challenge into a solution that is creative and effective.

Yes, as a coach, you are helping a client "hack their life."

Question #4: What is a coaching hack?

So far, we've painted a picture of people (coaches) who apply a mindset of developing relationships and using what they have to benefit others (coaching) in ingenious and efficient ways (hacks).

A coach helps a client(s) find the shortest–but–still-effective way to accomplish what they want, to hack their own life. But how? By using what I call *coaching hacks*. These are simple strategies that accelerate where a client is going and how fast they will get there. That's what fills the rest of this book, simple strategies to make every conversation more effective.

The rest of this book holds 31 ideas that will help you conduct your conversations in a coach-like manner. Each of the 31 ideas is designed to help you use what you've been giving to benefit someone else. Some of them will seem counterintuitive, but they work. Try them out. Experiment with them. Use them in your own words and your conversations.

Your role as a coach is to help someone else make sense of their world and to take action on it. These moments are prime targets for *coaching hacks*. This book focuses on the shortest possible route coaches can use to help their clients...Even if it's non-traditional. Don't you want to be more effective?

How to use this book

You've got some options for how to use this book, and there's no right way or wrong way. As I wrote, I realized that all I care about as you read is that you become more effective in your conversations. As long as that happens, it's all good.

But to make the most of what is in here, let me challenge you to *build habits*. Coaching gets much easier if you have solid practices on which you can fall back. You might think of creating healthy habits as the ultimate coaching hack.

What kind of habits? Things like:
- Letting the relationship do the work.
- Listening by default.
- Realizing you can't coach what your client won't say.

There are 44 coaching hacks in this book. You can either read from start to finish and go through all 44 in a row or pick and choose what is most helpful to you as you jump around. There's no right or wrong way to use what's in this book, as long as you integrate what you've learned to become more effective.

Every one of the coaching hacks follows the same format: A hack statement, a story about the hack, some suggestions for application, and a *What Now/Next* question.

- A hack comment: this is a one sentence summary of the big idea behind the coaching hack. It's supposed to be memorable!
- A hack story: Some background information, usually with a story that illustrates what the hack means and how you can use it.
- Suggestions for application: These are some ways where you might use what you've learned about the hack, and how it might come to life.
- What Now/Next question: Basically, this is the challenge to *do something* with what you've learned. These challenges point the way to turning these simple ideas into ongoing coaching habits.

Use the material in *Coaching Hacks* however it will benefit your coaching conversations. Highlight the stuff that stands out. Make notes in the margins. Refer back to it as a reminder. But go into reading with the understanding that application is the goal. This book exists to help you become more effective.

A word of warning: all the coaching hacks are inter-related so that it might seem like this book repeats itself. That is part of the design, as an illustration of how the hacks work together to make you more effective. Elegant pieces fitting together in a simple structure is a good way to think about it. If you get to a part that seems familiar, you can choose to read it for discovery or move to another part of the book

As you make your plan, remember: Coaching conversations come in three basic types:

- Informal: spur-of-the-moment conversations where the client may or may not know they're being coached.
- Formal: scheduled conversations where the client is clear that the time is for their benefit.
- Professional: Formal engagements including compensation for the coach.

Now let me be clear: reading and applying this book to your life will probably not make you a coach. It will get you started, and I hope it will challenge you to adjust how you handle every conversation you have! At the end of this book, we'll look at some next steps you can take if you want to complete the process of truly becoming a coach.

Each of the hacks is designed come to life in each of the three coaching types, but they'll look a little different in each environment. Remember that your goal is to turn these simple tricks into habits that make your conversations more effective.

Don't hesitate to make each hack your own. You'll get as much out of it as you put into applying each of these coaching hacks.

Coaching changes everything.

The best coaches listen by default, ask questions that produce forward momentum, and draw action steps out of their clients. Occasionally, a coach will offer some of their experience, but coaching clients always set the agenda. Coaches conduct the conversation so that the client chooses the way forward.

If you get good at doing the things that coaches do, your life gets easier.
- You'll develop the people around you.
- If you're a supervisor, you'll see that your entire team becomes more productive and efficient.
- If you're running your coaching practice, you'll see that your clients reach more of their goals.
- You get referred out more often.
- It will even become easier to have healthy, productive relationships in other parts of your life. Want an example? Your parenting!

In today's world, it's pretty rare to finds someone that puts others first. (Well other than coaches–and Jesus). The point of a coaching relationship is to ensure that the person you're working with gets where they want to go, and receives all the good stuff that comes with it.

In fact, committing to this mindset is an excellent way to distinguish yourself from other people. Use this as a career asset.

You might want to learn coaching skills. Combining generosity with coaching skills means you will make the people around you better. That is the difference between being a manager and a leader. Mastering this ability is a fast track skill. Want to move up in your organization? Make other people better. You'll be indispensable before you know it.

(Don't worry: *you'll* grow in every coaching relationship. But that's not the core purpose.)

That's really about all there is to it. Master these few ideas, and you too will be saying *coaching changes everything.*

How do you become a coach?

You start. You don't have to do anything or get prepared any particular way. Just start.

BUT...if you want to be a professional coach or even get paid to coach as a part of your living, there are best practices to embrace (like going to training and getting credentialed), and a few things to avoid. But mostly you just start.

Here's the challenge I have for you: get good at coaching. Good. Learn to do the things that active coaches do. A lot of the ideas in this book will take practice, so work at it. Integrate them into your life. Use these hacks to employ a repeatable process. It WILL make a difference.

You'll reread these words: *coaching changes everything.*

The Coaching Hacks

This is going to be fun. And helpful. Are you ready to get started?

There's a lot more than meets the eye going on in a coaching conversation. That's a fact. The coach is bringing their very best self to the conversation...And hopefully, the client is responding.

What seems small can make a huge difference. Pay attention to the details. Don't try to master all the coaching hacks at once, but pick out a few and integrate them into your conversations. You'll be more efficient, and your clients (or friends or co-workers or even your kids) will thank you.

So, here are 44 coaching hacks that you can use to make every conversation more effective!

Section 1: Building on a Solid Foundation for Coaching

Hack: Coaching is an intentional conversation with a focus leading to a relationship with a purpose.

Let's imagine you've got an important conversation on your calendar. You're thinking about this conversation for several days before it happens. Some part of your team's future rides on the outcome. How do you apply coaching hacks so that you get the maximum impact?

Coaching is an intentional conversation with a focus leading to a relationship with a purpose. Coaching happens in relationships, so multiple engagements make things happen.

Here's a summary of every coaching conversation in history:
- Take a snapshot of where you are.
- Develop a vision of where you want to be.
- Shorten the distance.

Sounds easy, right? But how? This simple framework defines coaching.

The beginning of the conversation might focus on exploring the current state of things. What's working and what might need to change.

The middle would dive into what things would be like if you were able to make those changes. You might even ask questions that help the other person picture the future when the ideas are realities.

The end would be all about mapping a route to move you from where you are now to the image you've developed. You wouldn't wrap up until you had an action plan on which you could immediately act. A coaching conversation is structured to ensure that the client chooses the way forward and takes does their work.

When you're using coaching hacks, you have several of these conversations. And suddenly your client is making real, measurable progress. That's what a coaching relationship is: a series of effective coaching conversations linked together.

The Key Habit: Discuss the differences between the current reality and what your client wants to have happen.

What Now/Next: How can you help the person you're talking with see the current state and a vision of the future side-by-side?

Hack: R + P + I = Coaching

There are lots of definitions of coaching. The International Coach Federation defines coaching as this: *partnering with clients in a thought-provoking and creative process that inspires them to maximize their personal and professional potential.*[1]

There's a lot there. Let's make it a little simpler. I was doodling on a legal pad one day and kept circling back to relationship and purpose and integration. Now, I went to school for engineering, and my father was a physicist, so I tend to like equations, statements or even diagrams that encapsulate the various parts into an elegant whole.

I just kept doodling, and eventually, it came together:

Relationship + Purpose + Integration = Coaching.

At CoachNet, we call this the core equation for coaching.

When you're using coaching hacks, add those three elements to get a particular kind of conversation: *a coaching conversation*. When you insert the specifics of your relationship to the purpose of the conversation and throw in some integrated coaching-style skills, you get a foundation for effective conversations.

But what do we mean by *relationship*? That's the personal bond between coach and the person(s) being coached. You must focus on the relationship first, and THEN you can add in coaching skills. It's a connection between people; analog or digital. You might even find yourself setting up your text message conversations this way!

As a side note, how you are in your relationships, in general, is how you are in your coaching relationships.

Here's what I mean by that: I am the kind of guy who diffuses tense situations with humor, not always appropriately. When I'm coaching, I have to guard against that because it's precisely when the tension rises that we can begin to make the kind of progress that clients look for in coaching. My natural tendencies show up in my coaching, even though in this case, it's not helpful!

Now, purpose. Simply, this is why you're talking to this person, or a clear statement of why the coaching relationship exists. When you're coaching, you have the chance to pre-select the results and growth you'll pursue. Meandering into any random topic doesn't help your client (or get you re-hired!). You have to be intentional.

At this moment you become a coach, by focusing on the client's success. However they happen to define it. You live in the client's world! Don't forget that.

Then finally, integration. As a coach, you can use all the tools you have available so that the relationship focuses on results and growth for the client. Your skills and mindset come to life. You might use that beginning, middle, end structure from a few pages ago. Do the things that coaches do as naturally as you possibly can! The basic coaching skills come to life. When you use coaching hacks, you commit to 1) listen deeply, 2) question boldly, and 3) challenge the client to act immediately.

All three of the phases support each other. If you fully commit to one, the other two flow naturally! And if you're missing one, then coaching is much more challenging. After all, that's how equations work! (And that's the end of the math lesson.)

The Key Habit: Monitor all three phases of the core equation for coaching to change the tone and outcomes of your conversations, and eventually, your relationships!

What Now/Next: Which of the three parts of the core coaching equation comes most naturally to you?

Hack: Get the relationship right. Then add coaching skills.

We've all got relationships. Some are healthy, and some aren't. Some are fun, and we look forward to connecting with that person. Some relationships just drain the energy right out of us. Those are the ones we have to decide whether we want to stay in!

Every relationship has potential to be a positive opportunity. Coaches make the most of those opportunities and do everything they can to develop relationships that matter.

When you're using coaching hacks, starting the relationship out on the right foot is crucial. The better you get at launching a relationship the right way, the more likely you'll be a competent coach.

The relationship matters. James Comer, a thought leader in education and change, says "No significant learning happens without a significant relationship."[2] So get it right, and the conversation will flow.

We must **get the relationship right. Then add coaching skills.**

Maybe it's a lifestyle of coaching, but I'd like to think of it as a life influenced by coaching skills...changed and informed by coaching skills.

Consider how these bullets shape the relationship between coach and client:
- Coaching is never about the coach. It's always about the client.
- Coaching is like a step ladder. It brings things into reach FOR YOUR CLIENT.
- The alongside component is key. That means peer-to-peer, adult-style learning is the preferred structure, instead of traditional teacher/instructor student classroom learning.
- The right relationship focuses the client on what they want to do and accelerates progress.
- What seems possible in a coaching relationship looks different in other situations. That's part of the power of coaching.
- Not everyone is coachable: commitment to change + relationship = coach- ability

So let's get practical. How do you launch a relationship the right way so that you can coach at the highest level?

Think about it as music. Music requires a relationship.

Someone plays or sings. Someone listens. Two equal parts with different roles and different responsibilities.

Without one portion of the relationship, the music is incomplete. Without the musician, there is no music. Without the listener, what did the music accomplish? Maybe it gave the player a chance to express something, but beyond that, there's not much going on.

For music to achieve the ultimate aim--to make people feel something--both participants in the relationship feed off each other. The listener welcomes the musician onto the stage or into the spotlight and invites them to offer something. The player shares their giftedness...the audience responds. The listener claps...the musician is inspired. It cycles like this in some pretty incredible ways--check out John Coltrane, BB King, Yo Yo Ma, Vince Gill or Kanye.

When you find an artist you like, you start to form a relationship with the artist. When it works, there's nothing like it.

With the advent of technology, relationships have a real chance to go both ways (from coach to client AND from client to coach). Without both parts, something is missing.

Starting with a question sets you up the same way. You invite the other person to offer something. When/if they do, you get to share your reaction, just like when you go listen to your favorite musician.

Coaching is much the same. The coach might welcome the person being coached with a question. The client offers something. The coach responds. The relationship takes off.

The Key Habit: Starting with a question changes things. I dream about that difference. You're forced to put yourself and your thoughts on the back burner and pay attention to the other person. You open yourself to a relationship. That takes nerve as well as skill.

What Now/Next: What would happen if you offered something in your next conversation, even an invitation for the other person to respond?

Hack: Always coach TOWARD something that the client chooses.

The most awkward moment I face in my coaching conversations looks like this recent example: We'll call my client Danny (not his real name). Danny has come to a moment of learning/self-realization. The lightbulb has gone off multiple times.

Then I have to drop the bomb. I get to ask Danny "How does this connect to the purpose of our coaching relationship?"

My stomach tightens up every time I ask this kind of question. My nerves become a jumble. There is no guarantee that the client will be able to connect what they're learning with why we're talking.

And when they can't...it is AWKWARD.

Asking a client to move away from the insights they are having and back to why they have a coach in the first place is never any fun...in the moment.

When you're using coaching hacks, this motion is what makes the difference between a tightly focused series of conversations and one that falls short of expectation. **Always coach TOWARD something that the client chooses.**

There's a reason why you're in this coaching relationship. What does your client want to accomplish? How will they be different after you've worked with them? These are just two of the things with which your client will need to wrestle.

In my experience, people who are interested in coaching relationships ask questions like these:

- Why aren't I more efficient? How can I become more effective?
- Who can I talk to about my situation?
- Where do I want to go?
- How can I decide what my next step(s) should be?
- How do I make the most of my opportunities?
- How can I manage my time more efficiently?
- How can you help me?
- How do I get unstuck?

Purpose in coaching relationships lives in the connection between small life changes and accomplishing the client's goals. Think about as Big Picture v. Small Picture.

- Big picture sees a measurable change toward the client's purpose.
- The small picture is how the client is living differently every day.

The enemy of purpose in coaching is a disconnect between small life change and big picture accomplishments/progress. When one doesn't set up the other, the relationship gets scattered.

This idea even helps the client who is all over the place. Some of my coaching clients only have a conceptual relationship with purpose. Helping a client connect what they're working on or changing in their lives (small picture) and what they want to accomplish (big picture) is often all the nudging needed to move them forward.

Managing this tension on-the-fly in coaching is a critical step to masterful coaching.

Sometimes you have to bottom line your client by asking a question like "What connection(s) do you see between the learning moment you just had and what we're here to accomplish?" I have to admit; I don't see the connection every time.

But as long as the client sees the connection and wants to pursue it, it's a viable coaching topic. The coach has to be aware of the tension, but the client has to actually and accurately make the connections come to life.

The Key Habit: Ask questions to help your client connect the focus of each conversation to the purpose of the larger coaching relationship.

What Now/Next: How do you keep your clients choose important coaching topics to make progress to their goals?

Hack: Use everything available to you to serve your client.

It will be different than all your other (non-coaching) relationships.

Remember how we defined a coach on the first page of this book: *A coach is someone who chooses to invest what they've been given to accelerate someone else's development or accomplishment.*

Integration is HOW a coach does this. Books written about the various kinds of coaching would fill several large book cases (coachnet.org/bibliography if you want to read more).

The best way to think about integration is to learn to access the mindset of a coach in coaching situations so that you can use the skills & tools in a way that's unique to you and your relationship. We'll dive into the specific skills in future hacks, but for now, think about it regarding The Arsonist v. The Firefighter.

Sometimes the coach has to be the arsonist...As you gain experience using coaching hacks, you learn when to start the conversation. You even get comfortable taking an appropriate risk. A single spark in the right place can launch a conversation that your client didn't see coming. Don't be afraid to strike a match, because if the relationship is right, the client will put the fire out. (There could be all kinds of reasons....remember trust the relationship. The client gets to choose the purpose.)

Other times the coach has to be the fireman. You also learn to risk when to put the conversation out. Think about a moment when the client can't connect the current conversation (small picture) to the purpose of the coaching relationship (big picture). Listen, so you're sure you're hearing what the client is saying and confirm the connection (or lack thereof). In those moments, open up the hose and douse the conversation. Again, if the relationship is right, the client will dry off and jump right back into coaching. You'll be ready with another question to re-start the conversation! **Use everything to serve your client.**

Remember, when you are using coaching hacks, you're always looking to benefit the client with your listening, your questions, and your experience!

The Key Habit: Use all your skills and experience to help the client opt for conversations that serve their bigger purpose!

What Now/Next: How will you know when to be a fireman and when to be an arsonist?

Hack: If nothing's changing, you're not coaching.

Coaching is fascinating, and working with coaches, is the fact that human beings don't make a decision--most of the time--unless they're nudged. We certainly don't change without the addition of some outside energy.

When you're using coaching hacks, you evaluate what is changing for the client as a direct result of your coaching! The fun part is that coaches get to be the nudge that results in change. **If nothing is changing, you're not coaching.**

The nudge can come from an impending deadline, accountability that matters, or even a big picture vision that is tied directly to the current decision.

I've seen this time and time again in my coaching. When a deadline is looming, my client makes choices that otherwise might be out of reach. Even if it's an obvious choice, the deadline nudges them forward.

Some folks need to be up against the wall. Other folks just need to know that the deadline is looming sometime shortly. The coach knows each client so that they can serve them most effectively.

Coaches can intentionally leverage this human tendency to increase effectiveness--or more accurately--the client's efficiency. How can you build helpful deadlines into your coaching conversations so that your client moves to action sooner rather than later?

One useful strategy is to just ask "How soon do you want this done?" or "What will finishing this do for you and your vision?"

Vision is the most powerful change agent in coaching. If you are working with a client who has an articulated purpose for being coached, it is an advantage for both coach and client to evaluate how every action plan connects to the larger purpose. When you use coaching hacks, you can keep your client's attention on how their vision will require them to change.

One of the hallmarks of my coaching practice is a side-by-side mapping of the initial situation the client is facing with a picture of the preferred new normal. This allows for an easy description of the road forward AND the specific naming of the measurable changes the transition process will require. I prefer to do this early in the coaching engagement.

In a recent coaching session, my client was envisioning how including an assessment in his team development would benefit the team, comparing the current state to their future. In every session, my client worked on growing team skills. A breakthrough moment came when the client could finally name the needed skills in crystal clear language.

He knew what it would take to develop the skill, but couldn't name how he would assess the current state of his team member's abilities in this area. That's where the assessment came in.

There was a reasonably large time commitment to learning to use the test and include it in his team's culture. The financial cost was high as well.

The first coaching question I asked was *"What will this information give you as the team leader?"* He talked for almost seven minutes listing the benefits.

I followed up with *"What reasons can you come up with to NOT learn and use the assessment?"* His only hesitation was the cost, but then said: *"I have the money and the time to do it."*

My next question was *"How will this help you accomplish the team's purposes?"* He had another long list of ways.

My final question was *"What would keep you from being trained?"* He immediately responded *"Nothing. I'm already on the registration site."*

The vision motivated him to act. It was powerful.

This kind of vision-related nudge works virtually every time. This particular client ended up choosing training that started two weeks later and had his team take the assessment before our next session.

The Key Habit: Nudge your client toward their vision and watch them choose the way forward!

What Now/Next: How will you know when to nudge your client toward their vision? What vision or deadline could you help your clients articulate and embrace in your next coaching session?

Hack: You can't coach what your client won't say.

In the first minutes of a coaching conversation, a coach will ask her client about the agenda for the discussion. "What do you want to talk about?" is a great opener. This is the beginning of negotiating the coaching agreement.

Every masterful coaching conversation works with three distinct coaching contracts:
- the purpose in the coaching relationship,
- the goals that indicate how the mission will happen and
- the specific outcomes for each session of the coaching relationship.

This last target should happen in every coaching conversation. That's one of the keys that separates good coaching from masterful coaching.

But nagging moments come up from time-to-time when the client puts something out there for the coaching agreement that just doesn't fit. You, as the coach, might have a sense that the client actually should work on something else. But the client is insisting that this is their topic.

What's a masterful coach to do?

When you're using coaching hacks, conversations are only as effective as the effectiveness of the conversational coaching agreement. Don't forget this always originates with the client. If they don't put it out there, you don't have it.

You can't coach what your client won't say.

Coaching conversations are under the client's control. They pick the topic, the measurements, the depth, even the pace.

Your role as a coach is to draw these things out of the client. The client should do the vast majority of the talking in every coaching conversation, so you have your work cut out for you.

If the client says it, you can't coach them toward it. In fact, if the client says it, you MUST coach them toward it. That's how coaching is different that other intentional relationships.

If the client DOESN'T say it, it's off the table... No matter how compelling a coach's instinct is about the topic.

Develop the coaching agreement, but make sure you're building around what the client says. Not what you hope they say or what you want them to say.

The Key Habit: A client has to say it before they can do it. You MUST coach what the client DOES say.

What Now/Next: Build your coaching agreements so that the client chooses the topic, the outcome and the measures for success.

Hack: Coaching & Mentoring are NOT the same thing.

The terms "coach" and "mentor" are ALMOST interchangeable, but the key word in that sentence is ALMOST. Potential clients have said any number of times over the years "I need a coach," and then a few minutes later "I need a mentor."

So which is it? **Coaching & Mentoring are NOT the same thing.**

Let's start with the big similarity: coaches and mentors have the same goal. Both want to see the client make progress toward their vision.

Don't miss this. **Being helpful as a coach or a mentor requires a vision.** Coaching hacks need one too. The person you're talking with is going somewhere, and you've got to be there to help!

The vision/challenge can be big or small. It might be long-term or short-term. Something you want to do by yourself or something that takes a team. Coaching hacks can apply in each of these cases. So might mentoring hacks, but that's a different book.

Both coaching and mentoring are most effective when you know where you want it to take you. There is a direct connection between clarity and progress. Like the old song says, "*If you don't know where you're going, any road will take you there!*"

Coaching and mentoring are intentional relationships. Since both roles have the same goal, the intention defines the interaction with the client. The key difference between coaching and mentoring is how the client's next step gets chosen. When you're using coaching hacks, those next steps are up to the client.

A mentor will offer you advice or guidance. They will tell you about things they've experienced and unpack how those things might apply to your life. **Mentors replicate skills in you that they have already learned.** It's almost as if they are cloning a small part of who they are--and how they are--in you. AND there's an expectation that you'll DO what the mentor suggests.

Coaches really won't do any of those things. **A coach will draw out of you what you know is inside of yourself but that you resist.** The coach will ask you a lot of questions and will patiently wait while you answer, even if it takes three or four tries. Coaches will help you connect the dots inside of your head, and then help you choose what action you want to take. The right coach will help you evaluate and apply the things you're learning about yourself.

When the coach offers an observation or a piece of guidance in coaching, the client evaluates it as objectively as possible. The follow-up actions are up to the client to choose....unless the coach is switching between coaching and mentoring (which happens all the time, despite what coaches will tell you!)

Someone who has both coaching and mentoring skills will teach you something when teaching is most effective. But they'll also step back and emphasize listening to help you make the connections or discoveries you need to make when that's the most appropriate strategy. Sometimes they'll pour in, and sometimes they'll draw out. In every situation, they should journey with you to wherever it is your vision is calling you.

When you've got an opportunity to use coaching hacks with someone, the first step is to get clear on what they are pursuing. "Where are you going?" you might ask.

The next step is deciding if they want a coach or a mentor. Maybe both sets of skills have valuable things to add.
- Sometimes you need someone who has been there and done that.
- Sometimes you need someone who has the kind of experience that you're seeking.
- Sometimes you need to just be with someone who's done something you're trying to accomplish yourself.

When experience matters, you need a mentor. Mentoring makes the biggest difference when the client prefers to work with someone who has been there and done that.

But...there are other times when the person wants to blaze new trails or go somewhere no one has gone before.

Or the most helpful thing might be to have someone who can just help you make sense of all the crazy thoughts running through your mind.

Still other times it's most useful to be able to push pause on someone and try to figure out *what's going on.*

Finding a coach or using coaching hacks might be the answer here. Coaching enhances every start up environment. You're often building the plane as you fly it, so the relationship that adds perspective is critical.

So, what's the vision your client is pursuing? And what kind of intentional relationship would be most helpful?

The Key Habit: Help the client see their vision and adapt how you show up to serve them.

What Now/Next: Journal about how your mentor presence will be different from your coaching presence. Reference the ICF's definition of Coaching Presence (ICF Competency #4) as a guide.

Hack: Coaching skills take about a MINUTE to learn, but a lifetime to MASTER.

The skills a coach uses are familiar: listening, questioning, and drawing out action steps from the client. In fact, these are skills that every healthy, functioning adult (and a lot of kids!) have at our fingertips.

Mike leads a team at his church that has sometimes struggled to be productive. He has commented to me that he's not sure how he's helping his staff be so much more productive. "My one-on-ones and my team meetings just flow so smoothly, that they can't be making THAT much difference." Mike is now using coaching hacks.

He told me that WHAT he does with them hasn't changed, but the ORDER of what he does is different.

"I still ask the same amount of questions, but now there's a structure and logic behind what I'm asking," Mike says. "My team makes much better decisions and better plans. It's enjoyable to work here now, and I'm convinced that I want to be an excellent coach."

Coaching skills take about a MINUTE to learn. And a lifetime to MASTER. It's not that the skills require new learning, but rather it's key to understand when to use which skill.

Think of it like playing an instrument. Within a few lessons, you can play every note. But does that mean you can jam? Not likely.

Over time, with practice, you learn when to play which note. And maybe just as important, you learn when NOT to play. The same applies to coaching.
When you're using coaching hacks, you master WHEN to ask that question. Even though we listen to the people around us every day, getting into the world where they live is a big challenge.

It's not as easy as it sounds. It takes discipline, focus, and intention. Mixing art and science makes it work. That's why there's a difference between using coaching hacks and becoming a coach. Everyone can use coaching skills, though not everyone can become a coach.

The Key Habit: Focus on the skills you already have, but use them in a different order than you typically do!

What Now/Next: What do you think you are best at doing? Listening, questioning or drawing out action steps?

Section 2: How to Think Like a Coach

Hack: Listen 80% of the time. Talk 20%.

At the core, the joke from the introduction to this book has some significant truth. Every coaching conversation in history follows the same basic pattern
- The client figures out where they are.
- The client pictures where they want to be.
- The client takes action to shorten the distance between those two points.

But what is the coach doing during all this activity? Using coaching hacks means applying a variation of the Pareto Principle to structure conversations.

You've probably heard of the 80-20 rule. Wikipedia describes it like this:
The Pareto principle (also known as the law of the vital few, or the principle of factor sparsity) states that, for many events, roughly 80% of the effects come from 20% of the causes. Management consultant Joseph M. Juran suggested the principle and named it after Italian economist Vilfredo Pareto, who noted the 80/20 connection while at the University of Lausanne in 1896, as published in his first paper, "Cours d'économie politique." Pareto showed that approximately 80% of the land in Italy belonged to 20% of the population; Pareto developed the principle by observing that about 20% of the peapods in his garden contained 80% of the peas[3]

This balance comes to life in coaching as well. When you're using coaching hacks, 80% of the progress a client makes comes when the coach is listening. Only 20% of client progress comes when the coach is talking.

You read that right: **Listen 80%. Talk 20%.** Using coaching hacks means listening another person into change.

Masterful coaches invest time and energy into actually hearing what the other person is saying and helping them discovers what is most important. You partner with the client and build trust. Using summary, reframing and restating helps you work on a surface issue and a deeper root cause.

Here's a guideline: Always listen a little bit longer than is comfortable.   It's stunning how often I find myself leaping ahead in my mind, maybe thinking about my next question, and missing what the other person is saying to me. Giving the gift of focused attention is a multiplier. You'll get farther faster, just by demonstrating to the other person that you think what they say is valuable!

But how? What if your mind is always wandering? Use this simple two step process: First, get the facts right and repeat them back to the other person. Second, ask the person to dive under the surface and look for causes. The 80-20 balance focuses you.

Listening is a powerful tool. In almost every coaching situation, the person being coached will tell you what is going on. That doesn't mean that you'll hear it. That's why getting the facts right starts the process. Then you can get under the hood and into what is going on.

The Key Habit: Commit to listening to your client until you can see what they see.

What Now/Next: What relationship(s) do you have that you could set up for action? What could you listen for in your next conversation with that person?

Hack: Coaching gets the client into motion.

My client was stunned. "I just brought up this terrible thing that happened to me when I was 11, and you didn't ask me ANYTHING about it. What kind of coach are you?"

"Well, that's just it. I'm a *coach*. If you want to talk about what happened to you years ago, I'm not your guy," I said. "Coaches don't do that. In fact, I'm pretty sure I can't help you deal with that."

These moments happen to every coach, but they're not the client's fault. It usually stems from a misunderstanding of what coaching is designed to do. Coaches don't help process what's happened in the past, but rather build current understanding for future impact.

When you use coaching hacks, LEVERAGE backward reflection, but don't forget that's a tool and not an outcome. Outcomes become realities when the client does something. **Coaching gets the client into motion.**

Think about the significant accomplishments of your life. Getting married. Landing that promotion. Becoming clear on what you're called to accomplish. Parenting your son or daughter through a particularly challenging time. Did you talk about what you wanted to happen before you did it? Or did you do something and process whether you got what you wanted?

Most of the time I suspect you thought about it, maybe talked to someone else, and the did something. That's the key paradigm for coaching: *conversation first, then action.*

Using coaching hacks means that the other person walks away from your conversation with a clear action plan about what they're going to do next. Get them moving!

The Key Habit: The hardest part of helping someone get started is choosing (and taking) one bold step.

What Now/Next: In your next conversation, help the other person choose a bold step they can take. Something they can do that will make a difference.

Do it one step at a time. Here's the thing about bold steps: they get accomplished with a bunch of tiny little steps.

Hack: The best questions produce forward momentum.

Coaches are known for their ability to ask questions. The International Coach Federation (ICF) even lists one of the core coaching competencies as "Powerful Questioning."

Take a look at the how the ICF defines this competency: *"the ability to ask questions that reveal the information needed for maximum benefit to the coaching relationship and the client."*[4] That's a great goal…To always ask the kind of question that gets to what is most important. But don't stop there. Maximum benefit means that the client can take some action that moves them closer to their goal!

The best questions produce forward momentum.

In fact, in our training at CoachNet, students often ask us for lists of powerful questions that they can use to help the client come to the point of breakthrough. That's a great temptation, but notice how the competency is named: it's *powerful questioning*, NOT powerful questions.

When you're using coaching hacks, you learn to ask the right question to the right person at the right time. They get going toward what they want. It's an active, on-going posture that distinguishes a coaching question.

Here's a simple acronym I like to use as a guardrail to keep my questioning on track: Always ask **BOLD** questions.
- **B:** Your questions should *build forward momentum* or *break a negative slide*.
- **O:** Structure your questions, so they are *open ended for new possibilities*.
- **L:** After you've asked a question, always *leave the room so the client can think* before answering.
- **D:** And your questioning should help the client *dive to action*.

Each one of the four keys adds a little power to what your question might create. Leaving even one of those out, short circuits what your question can do. It's almost a disservice to your client.

Using your questions to explore where your client is going keeps them focused on what they want to accomplish. They almost can't help moving toward a new future! That's what it means to build forward momentum!

It's so tempting to ask about the details of something that happened or to explore a childhood memory, but how often does this build forward momentum? Using coaching hacks to make your conversations more productive usually means leaving your client with a sense of where they're going, not where they've been. Moving to somewhere they want to go is why people work with coaches in the first place.

The Key Habit: Balance listening and asking questions! You've been asking questions your whole life, now leverage them for forward momentum!

What Now/Next: How will you keep your questions focused on the future? How will you resist the urge to ask about the past?

Hack: Every bold question has more than one answer.

My small business coach Mark LeBlanc says "I like to live in a world where every question has more than one answer."

But for most of us, we have definite preferences. We like it when it's simple, even binary or either/or. Anytime we can choose between two options; we are prone to choosing the path of least resistance. Easy visualization of the road forward appeals to our brains. Without thinking, we tend to make one option in front of us better than the other. We ignore entire sets of options that are within our reach.

Coaches need to understand that pattern and be equipped to handle whatever option the client chooses. **Every bold question has more than one answer.**

When you use coaching hacks, your job is to nudge your client away from the simple, clear, easy answer. Every bold question you ask should create space for the client to explore something that is unfamiliar, or even daunting. A breakthrough often results, pointing the client toward something that wasn't on their radar

Buddhists and Christian mystics like Richard Rohr call this non-dualistic thinking. We move away from either/or to both/and. We get to live with the tension of having to find our way forward, evaluating all the potential influences along the way.

F. Scott Fitzgerald wrote something similar: "The test of a first-rate intelligence is the ability to hold two opposed ideas in mind at the same time and still retain the ability to function."
[5]The coach aims to invest time and effort to help the client grab onto the two options and explore the space in-between. This time is challenging, but not wasted.

Consider the polarities you might encounter in a coaching conversation:
- Good Ideas v. Bad Ideas
- Healthy Relationship v. Unhealthy Relationship
- Effective Strategy v. Ineffective Strategy.

Or some of the more challenging ones:
- Results v. Growth.
- Luggage (the things you choose to take with you into a relationship) v. Baggage (the things you bring whether you want to or not)
- Shrewd v. Foolish

But it's also effortless for the coach to lead the client to what you want them to explore. Resist that urge. The great gift of coaching is that when we're in a relationship, we're better at choosing which idea serves us more efficiently.

The Key Habit: Help the client to define the extremes, then explore the third way in between.

What Now/Next: Ask your client what the best/worst case scenarios are. Then help them find the realistic third way!

Hack: If a question doesn't inspire action, ask a different one.

My first career was a television news reporter. I used to be the guy standing outside of the courthouse or alongside the massive 27 car pileup, trying to paint a picture with words about what happened there and why it mattered to the viewer.

Sometimes it was easy because I covered some pretty big events--like elections. Other times it was hard because abandoned buildings on fire or a giant cow sculpture made entirely out of butter (both actual stories I covered) just don't have much big picture meaning.

When I became a coach, the dialogue changed. When using coaching hacks, rather than describing things that have already happened, conversations start centering on things that have not yet happened.

Do you see the difference? My two careers have demonstrated to me that conversation and action are linked. In fact, one doesn't typically happen without the other. *But the order in which those two things happen matters.* When you use coaching hacks, continually evaluate whether the action already happened, or if it's something to investigate in the future. **If a question doesn't inspire action, ask a different one.**

Coaching conversations leverage both approaches. Often a coach will start by helping another person understand what's going on around them. Then that conversation continues as the client decides what to do about their current situation. It's a conversation that starts with action AND leads to action. This example is conversation THEN action.

Other coaching conversations follow an event or activity. The initial action happens BEFORE the conversation takes place. Coach and client debrief what happened and look for learning that came from the conversation.

Both conversation and action need to be present, but either option can come first.

Conversation   Action

Figure 1 Conversation-Action Loop

There will be times when something happens, and you just have to talk about it.

But there will be other times when deciding what to do and talking about what will occur in the future is more helpful.

The key approach is *"Which one do you think is more useful to the person I'm working with?"*

Here are some hack-like ideas you can use to structure your conversations, depending on where your client wants to start the conversation:

Conversation First, then Action:
- Helps a person determine their course of action and timetable.
- The client takes a future-orientation and talks through decision-making, relational health, and who will be affected by the decision.
- Facilitates noticeable and distinct change.
- The larger the action, the higher ceiling the conversation can have!
- Open ended questions that open up possibilities are the key.

Action First, then Conversation:

- Actions get completed so the conversation can focus on understanding and emotion.
- A deeper understanding of what has already happened is the goal.
- Helps a person understand the details and meaning of a situation.
- If there are learnings, the other person likely changes what they do next.
- Closed ended questions that confirm what the person is thinking can be a helpful tool.

The Key Habit: Understand that effective conversations come in two forms, but always result in action.

What Now/Next: Spend some time in personal reflection about whether conversation or action comes first when you're most effective.

Hack: Get the facts right. THEN go beneath the surface.

Medical professionals talk about both treating symptoms and curing causative issues. For example, when you have a headache, do you take aspirin to relieve the pain? Or would a massage to reduce the tension that is causing the headache be a better strategy?

When you're using coaching hacks, you have to make the same kind of decision. For example, do we work with a client to eliminate the problem of being double-scheduled today? Or, do we focus on an overall time management strategy? That's presenting symptom (being double-scheduled) v. root cause (improved time management).

Getting to the core of an issue starts with understanding that there is a difference between listening & hearing. **Get the facts right, THEN go beneath the surface.**

Hearing is allowing the information to enter your mind. You know it's registering, but that's where it ends. It's a passive process.

Listening is taking in the input, and then intentionally working to treat it so that it becomes something useful. Listening is an active process. You have to invest time and energy to ensure you're getting the facts right, but also helping your client discover the meaning of those events.

But even more, there are two kinds of listening: active and reflective.

Reflective listening ensures the coach works to get the facts right and helps the client discover what they mean, often by feeding back what the client has said).

Active listening helps the client connects the dots for themselves, and gives plenty of space for unexpected discoveries.

Neurologically, when a client knows the coach is listening, their brain makes connections it otherwise wouldn't. That's the root of insight and sets the stage for discovering what matters to your client.

Remember the difference between listening for a root cause and listening for a symptom. Coaches sometimes hear meanings that are only apparent in between the words jump out. You can even "see" underneath the facts of the overall message. The deeper meaning is within reach for coach and client.

When you get stuck coaching, default back to listening. More questions won't help, more actions won't help. More listening will.

The Key Habit: Develop these keys for listening:
- Accurately take in the input.
- Process it and manage your thoughts, feelings, and reactions.
- Give plenty of space so the client can come to their conclusions.

What Now/Next: Pay attention to your next conversation to when the topic is a presenting symptom and when it's a root cause of the client's situation.

Hack: Always draw out the client's discoveries. Drawing out sets the client free to act.

Michelangelo, the sculptor, is quoted as saying "Every block of stone has a statue inside it and it is the task of the sculptor to discover it.[6]

This same discovery mindset works for a coach. Picture an artist circling a block of stone, trying to imagine the statue inside. When you're using coaching hacks, you engage the client looking to help them discover the work of art inside them.

Maybe we even try to picture items hidden inside the situation. But the most efficient posture helps the CLIENT picture the work of art in the case. You get the privilege of drawing out what's already there.

When you use coaching hacks, assuming that the other person needs something you have is dangerous. The other person already has everything they need to be successful. Your role is to help them discover it. Inside of the coaching relationship. Your conversations will be the most useful when you put your energy into helping your client name and articulate what's going on inside of them. **Drawing out sets the client free to act.**

We're not there to fix anything (or anyone), or to demonstrate how smart we are. We're there to help the client connect the dots on what they have going on and to conduct the conversation so that the hidden becomes clear and easily seen. Commit to drawing wisdom out of your client. It's fun! Over time, you'll notice that you can change the other person's perspective, just by showing up.

Using coaching hacks means that we're not fixing anything...Or any one. Coaches get into trouble when they try to repair the client or views a client as someone/something to be fixed.

The Key Habit: Remember Michelangelo. Learn to help your client discover what's inside them and draw it out.

What Now/Next: Practice on yourself. What's a realization you're having about yourself that you can tell someone about?

Hack: The potential power of a question is inversely proportional to its length.

Back to my first career was as a radio host and newsman. It's a great job, and I loved doing it. Maybe the best part was getting to interview people that I would have no way to talk with in any other circumstance.

I got to ask B.B. King "How do you practice?" Al Gore had to answer "Why do you want to be President?", and Michael Jordan discussed, "What keeps you on top?"

What do you notice about those questions? The longest one is seven words.

If the 80-20 rule for coaching applies and extra details distract the client, short questions are better questions.

Your quick questions give the client the maximum space to think and come up with their answers. That's the goal. **The potential power of a question is inversely proportional to its length.**

When you use coaching hacks, one of your strategies is to help the client process out loud whatever they're thinking or feeling. It's a guided process, for sure, but your mindset should be to bring the client's inner monologue out into the open.

Human beings come up with their most creative answers when the voice in our heads is on display for someone we trust. The combination of listening and questions makes this happen. In fact, the coach plugs into the client's world so that only the client can answer the questions the coach asks.

Here's a little score sheet I use. It follows a simple question evaluation framework:

Closed >> open >> specific >> personal

Figure 2 - Evaluate Your Questions

The scoring goes like this:

- A closed (yes/no) question gets -1 point. We don't want to ask those unless we're confirming something the client is saying. That's the only place for a closed ended question. An example is "Do you have more to say?"

- An open-ended question gets one point. These questions expand the client's thoughts and remove any limits the client might be hiding. They also require thought to answer. You might say "What else is on your mind?"

- Specific questions include the client's context. Anyone could potentially answer specific questions, but they factor in what's going on around the client. Try questions like "Who else sees this situation as you do?" These questions get 2 points.

- Personal questions are open ended, factor in the client's context and can ONLY be answered by the client. They usually begin with "What." These questions might touch on the emotions the client is feeling, and they might cause the client to see their situation differently. They might even see themselves differently. These are what we're after, and these questions get 3 points, and a bonus point if they begin with "What." Watch for your chance to ask a short question like "What do you want now?" or "What action can only you take?"

- Bonus scoring rule: Take one point away for each question that is longer than eight words. Add one bonus point for a particular question or personal question that is less than five words.

A full coaching session builds around solid, powerful questions will score in the 20s or 30s. That's giving your client a lot of room to think about what's most important! It's harder to do than you think!

When the coaching conversation is going well, every question builds on the last, and your client makes more progress than you could have imagined!

The Key Habit: Keep your questions short. Seven words or less is a real target.

What Now/Next: Practice asking questions that only take you a few words to ask, without ANY extra details.
- If you need to, listen back to a recorded conversation and write down every word you say. THEN go back and try to make every question shorter.

- Then take the short questions, and see if you can do it again. Repeat this process a third time if you can. Call this word economy, and it will make every single conversation more productive. It's a powerful coaching hack.

Hack: The best questions require no setup or explanation.

My client was struggling. We had taken 4 or 5 different passes at where he wanted to go. His effort was there, and long pauses began to open up between the ends of my questions and the beginnings of his answers.

I felt a knot growing in my stomach during those pauses. I wanted to jump into the conversation. About half the time, I resisted. Sometimes adding extraneous details to the question was just too attractive, and I gave in.

Every time I dressed up a question with an explanation or some details I thought were useful, my client struggled to answer. When I just put it out there, short and to the point, the answers and ideas flowed out of my client. You make your questions as powerful as possible.

When you are using coaching hacks, you leave out all the extra details.

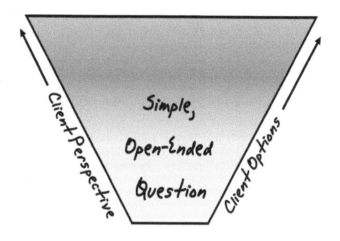

Figure 3 -- What happens when you ask open ended questions.

The best questions require no setup or explanation.

When you ask your question directly, without any additional details, you give space to open your client's perspective. Without any extra effort, you make the client the hero of their own story, and they can see options they might miss otherwise.

You don't need to show what you know or demonstrate your understanding. In fact, it doesn't matter if you understand your client.

My brother Tom is a lawyer. Occasionally when he is writing a legal brief, we'll have a five-minute coaching session. Now, I know NOTHING about the law. I stick to focused questions, about what he's trying to accomplish. Usually, within 3 or 4 inquiries, he says "I've got it!" and hangs up the phone. I NEVER know what the call was about, but the coaching hacks make the conversation worthwhile!

You work against your client when you throw in extra thoughts or try to explain your question. Every detail limits the client's perspective and narrows the options they can access.

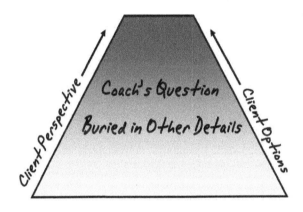

Figure 4 -- Bad Things Happen When You Add Details

Effective conversations help the other person come to conclusions that they would miss otherwise. Your presence is necessary, but their thinking is even more important! Don't let your client off the hook—they benefit from wrestling with the details of their situation.

The Key Habit: Leave out all the details in the questions you ask.

What Now/Next: Practice asking questions without ANY extra details.

Hack: The backstory is not your friend.

The single most common mistake a new coach makes is to spend too much time listening to things that happened in the past.

One client of mine was going through a difficult period in her leadership. She was clearly in charge, but her team was starting to give her some problems. We were spending a tremendous amount of time going over everything that happened since our last conversation. We weren't getting to what the conversation was about until 40 minutes into a 60-minute call. That only left 20 minutes to make the progress she wanted.

Finally, I had enough. I remember asking: "What's the big challenge you're facing this month?" I had to ask several times to get her to answer. Her emotions needed some time and space, and I didn't see how it was serving the relationship. I had done her a disservice letting that processing take up our work time.

When I was a younger coach, I made this mistake fairly often. Then it occurred to me that I was letting her remain trapped in the past (which she couldn't do anything about) instead of inviting her to work on the future (which she could shape). Living in the past, or even talking about it too much, doesn't move the relationship forward. We had to get away from what had already happened and focus on what was GOING to happen. **The backstory is not your friend.**

When you use coaching hacks, you avoid the past and work to move the story forward, on whatever path the other person chooses.

If a client is clinging to a backward-looking view, coaches explore the reason(s) the past is so compelling. If you need to, you can let the client vent to manage the emotions within a story. That's powerful. But don't let it take over the entire conversation!

The Key Habit: Keep the client looking to what they can affect (the future) and avoid too much conversation about what they can't (the past).

What Now/Next: Challenge your client to look beneath the surface of the critical issue, and guide them away from the past.

Hack: Clients in motion tend to stay in motion (and other rules of motion).

Sir Isaac Newton broke new ground in virtually everything he took on. The famous story about watching the apple fall from the tree and wondering whether there was a force pulling the fruit down to the ground was only the first thing on his list of accomplishments. He was the first one to come up with a description of what was going on in gravity.

- Newton also invented the telescope, developed calculus, explained how the planets moved around the sun and explored how colors fit together in the prism. When I read about people like Newton, I sometimes feel like I've wasted my life. Can you relate?

Newton also wrote three laws that explain how objects move. His three laws of motion are:

1. Objects at rest or objects in motion tend to stay at rest or in motion unless acted on by an outside force.
2. Force equals mass times acceleration. Force is what causes an object to change direction.
3. For every action, there is an equal and opposite reaction.

When you use coaching hacks, you see applications of these same laws that determine client action(s).

Bottom line, **clients in motion tend to stay in motion.** Even a little progress is worth celebrating. The coach's reaction should be a celebration to all progress (but be sure that your response is proportionate to the progress your client is making).

There are three different kinds of motion in a coaching conversation, and there are hack-style reactions from the coach for all of them.

The three types of motion are:

- **Actions:** what gets done between now and the next coaching conversation.
- **Plans:** what gets done between the first coaching session and when the coaching relationship ends.
- **Growth:** what the client learns about themselves that allows them to repeat the results of the coaching relationship without input from the coach.

When you're working with coaching hacks, you are trying to build capacity or ability in the client. You don't want to have to repeat the content of the coaching relationship because the client is dependent on your input to make progress!

The Key Habit: Celebrate the progress your client is making, but don't overdo it to the point where your client loses trust in your integrity.

What Now/Next: Work on ways to compliment your client when they make progress toward their goals or complete their actions!

Section 3: Using Coaching Hacks in Your Conversations

Hack: Coaches make the client the hero of the story, not themselves.

My client Dominic came into our scheduled conversation without a plan (which is a no-no in coaching). He didn't have any topic ideas. So I took a typical coach's posture and asked him "What ideas do you have for our time?"

Dominic: *I'm not at all sure.*

Jonathan: *Well, what comes to mind when you think about how we could invest this time?*

Dominic: (long pause) *Well...* (another long pause...)

Jonathan: (waiting in silence)

Dominic: *Boy, I'm just not sure.*

Jonathan: *What challenges are you facing right now?*

Then Dominic was off. He brainstormed about 15 things, one right after another. His tone of voice changed as he mentally sorted his challenges into things he could conquer, and things he didn't.

He wanted to focus on the things he could conquer, and I was happy about that. Over the next 30 minutes, we separated them into 3-4 categories: Urgent & Important, Urgent But Not Important, Important But Not Urgent, and Not Important Nor Urgent.

Inside my head, I began to panic, and question my coaching ability. I had to work to not insert my insecurities and drive Dominic somewhere he didn't want to go. I kept asking him *"What else?"* and *"Where do we go from here?"* But even still, it felt like we were flying blind, and coaching without a clear path.

It was brutally difficult, and the voice in my head just got louder and louder the longer the conversation went on.

53 minutes into a 60-minute conversation, we finally came to a place where he said: *"I know what I want to work on."*

By this time, my inner voice was telling me to turn in my credential and never coach again. I forced myself to ask, *"Where do we start?"* He answered with some concrete next steps. *"What do you want out of this conversation?"* was my next question.

Dominic paused again. 55 minutes into the conversation. He said, *"I need to decide what order to do the Urgent and Important things."*

Before I could say a word, he continued *"And the order is..."* Dominic then laid out his next two weeks of work, ending with *"This has been the best session we've ever had!"* And we had been working together for four years! It didn't feel to me like this was a perfect session at all, but Dominic was over the moon.

When you're using coaching hacks, your challenge is to make the other person the hero. An excellent strategy to do this is to build your coaching conversations around the client's story(s). Think about the coaching session with Dominic. Who was the hero? (Hint: it wasn't the guy who considered turning in his coaching credential.)

Here's a confession: I prefer it when my client comes into the conversation with some clarity about what they want to do in our session. But how many conversations in real life have that kind of focus?

Then there's the fact that people process ideas differently. Some clients can get right to the point. Other clients default to choosing 10,000 words when 100 might do. The challenge for the coach is to maintain a high level of relationship and to stick with what the client wants to accomplish, regardless of his/her preferred communication style.

Every compelling story has a beginning, a middle and an end where something distinct happens. At the start of a coaching story, you meet the characters and gain an understanding of the situation you're there to address. Clarity drives at the initiation of the overall coaching relationship, or the beginning of each coaching conversation.

In the middle of the story, conflict or tension grows. You and your client might be getting to a deeper understanding of the root of the issue, or the client might be able to talk about it with you because you've built enough trust. There could even be surprises along the way.

At the end of the story arc, the resolution comes. The tension/conflict is taken care of, and the client can point to what is different in them because of coaching. Whether there is a happy ending is less important than whether the client feels like there has been the right kind of progress. In this case, resolution=progress=success. Always evaluate through the client's lens.

At each stage of the story, the coach has an opportunity to help the client see themselves as the hero. The best coaches tailor each coaching conversation to where the client sees themselves in the larger story—the beginning, the middle or the end.

- Are you at the beginning? Ask the client what you might need to know to coach well?
- Are you seeing signs of developing conflict (the middle of the storyline)? Ask what is causing the conflict and explore potential solutions.
- Are you nearing resolution? Ask the client what would multiply the impact of the results they're anticipating.

. You can dig deeper, and get at the core of the issue—whatever that issue is—and help the client develop their long-term results. They can conquer! And conquering heroes don't just grab band aids for whatever presenting symptoms happen to be in front of them.

The Key Habit: Look for opportunities to help your client ensure that they see themselves as the hero of the story.

What Now/Next: How can you take the time to listen to your client's hero story? For what, specifically, are you listening? Develop a strategy to dig beneath the surface of what you're working on with your client(s). That's where you find what will make them a hero!

Hack: The client ALWAYS gets to choose.

We've been journeying together through the Coaching Hacks for a while. And I have a confession. I hope you're sitting down.

I'm not a natural coach. It's all learned behavior for me.

In fact, I am a recovering consultant.

I LOVE to tell people what to do. My original wiring demands to talk. My brain fires when I think you're asking for my guidance or direction. I like being the hero that rides in from somewhere else and points out what I see.

But it's not helpful in light of my commitment to coaching. The client is the hero of every story, and we're on the client's journey. When you use coaching hacks, it requires an entirely different orientation toward what you get to talk about with your client. The client ALWAYS gets to choose. Coaching and consulting differs here.

Lots of coaches struggle not to consult. It's especially difficult if you have experience and success in the field where you coach. You KNOW what it takes. You fight the temptation to share your experience when you should be drawing out of your client.

When you're using coaching hacks, you commit to ensuring that your client gets to choose the topic and the direction in every conversation. You even give your client the option to choose what they do with any input or insight you might offer them.

Masterful coaches call this the *coaching agreement*. It's so important that the International Coach Federation wrote a particular competency about the idea. It reads like this:

Establishing the Coaching Agreement—Ability to understand what is required in the specific coaching interaction and to **come to agreement** with the prospective and new client about the coaching process and relationship.

If your client is choosing where the conversation is going to go, you are along for the ride. A robust framework for ensuring that you stay out of consultant mode is asking questions that draw out three things:
- The broad topic of conversation, which eventually leads to

- the core issue to address, and
- Helps the client identify what they want to take away from this conversation (their measures for success).

Think of these like an onion. Pull away one layer at a time until you get to the core the client wants to take away from the conversation.

In a recent coach training session, Nathan said "I've started to call this process 'The Coach's Drill.' You just keep going deeper until you find the core issue the client has as their focus and begin to help the client identify how they want to address it!"

A few minutes later as he was giving feedback to one of his class mates, he said "Get out the Coach's Drill!!!!!! Drill baby! Drill!"

You drill for the core issue and the measures for success! And don't forget, you're not going to know what they are, but your client will!

The Key Habit: Let the client choose what they want to talk about, and when they have what they want out of the conversation.

What Next/Now: Ask questions like "What do you want to talk about?" and "How will you know you've been successful?" in the early stages of the conversation.

Hack: You MUST coach what the client DOES say.

(All of the names and few other identifying pieces of information in the following have been changed to protect the ridiculous.)

One of my clients had a problem staff person. We'll call my client Ronnie, and her staff person Tim. Tim just had his way of doing things, and it drove Ronnie crazy. Nuts.

At least once a week, Ronnie swooped in and did or re-did some part of Tim's job.

When it came time for our coaching session, Ronnie was complaining that the problem had gotten worse and not better every time she swooped in. Tim just took more and more advantage of the situation. I knew in a matter of moments what the issue was, but it seemed to be just out of reach for Ronnie.

Ronnie, in fact, WAS the problem.

With about ten questions, the light bulb went on for Ronnie. She realized that there are only a few things in Tim's job that had prescribed procedures. The majority just had to be done.

"I'm trying to control what and how Tim does his job, and I shouldn't do that," she said.

For a few minutes, my questions focused on what lived beneath the control process. But Ronnie wasn't interested in looking at the causes of her behavior; she was only open to brainstorming new ways to get Tim to do things her way. All Tim had to do was see things Ronnie's way and all would be right with the world.

She wanted to focus on ways to get him to see this as the key to their working relationship.

So...

YOU may want to dig deep, but if THE CLIENT doesn't...

YOU may want to talk about some particular issue, but if THE CLIENT doesn't...

YOU may see a great set of options, but if THE CLIENT doesn't...The conversation just isn't going to go there.

When you use coaching hacks, the list of places where you can't go can get long pretty fast. Because **you MUST coach what the client does say.** You don't do the work for your client, but you set them up to make their own decisions and take their actions.

Here's the crazy part: when you see it on paper, it sure reads like it doesn't work–or it CAN'T work–but it does. Coaching works like nothing else. Because what the client does say often leads to lasting change.

Even if the coach has some other idea about what would be helpful, the client still gets to choose.

The Key Habit: Resist the urge to re-direct the conversation to your ideas and priorities.

What Now/Next: Make a list of things people typically ask you about and brainstorm ways to draw out what another person might want to talk about in those areas.

Hack: Meet The CHAIN: A repeatable map can maximize the impact of your conversations.

A few years ago, my office monitor got covered in post-it notes. All around the rim, one note after another was stuck on top of the next. Each note has one coaching question that I had asked in some coaching situation. If the question drew a meaningful response from the client, I wrote it down and stuck it on the monitor.

Over a couple of years, the 50 or so notes accumulated had stopped being helpful. Navigating through all the little pieces of paper stuck on my monitor became impossible. Even a part of the screen got obscured by the collage of coaching questions.

When I was first starting as a coach, a feeling of being overwhelmed was not uncommon. There are a lot of pieces swirling in a coaching conversation, and I struggled to keep them working together. My post-it notes overload didn't help. I needed a simpler strategy and had to keep my attention on the right things.

What I needed was to engage a conversational system. A *consistent* system moves you closer to the outcome(s) you want. A repeatable conversation map is an example of a system. You do the same things over and over again, and if you've got the right one, you should be functioning in a way that develops the people around you.

In your next few conversations, focus on two things: 1) what YOU do/say to the other person and 2) the results your actions generate. You can't get caught up in how the other person will respond because it's unpredictable and out of your control. Put your energy into places where you can affect.

When you use coaching hacks, it's most effective to deploy the same structure in several consecutive conversations. This tool maximizes the impact of your consistent communications.

Here's the simple road map we teach in Integrated Coach Training:
- **C**onnecting
- **H**earing
- **A**rticulating
- **I**mplementing
- **N**oticing

You'll notice that it's a simple acronym: CHAIN. The next few hacks go into more detail about each phase. The CHAIN is an organic road map to show connecting conversations one after another.

The most common CHAIN illustration is a drawing that looks like this:

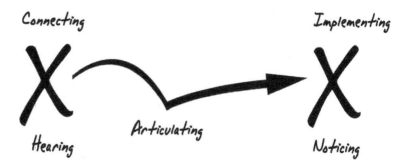

Figure 5 -- The CHAIN Model

Finding an easy way to join conversations makes you more productive and helps the client get where they want to go efficiently. Similarly structured conversations sequence together more quickly. The most effective coaches use a model to ensure maximum impact.

Picture a strand of DNA, which is organic and unique to every individual. The two strands of a DNA double helix are intertwined...Rather like the relationship between coach and client (aimed at a purpose) in coaching. Using a map like this is a way to structure a conversation to ensure that the client takes their action. An effective coaching relationship is simply a bunch of productive conversations linked together.

Remember the keys for coaching: Listen to where the other person is, help them see where they'd like to be, and then shorten the distance between those two points. Work one step at a time. But a word of caution: don't overthink it. Trust the coaching process. Use your coaching hacks.

The Key Habit: Choose or develop a roadmap that you can consistently follow in your conversations.

What Now/Next: Explore the CHAIN model to see if it fits in your natural conversational style.

Hack: Connecting. Coaching is a relational connection built on transparency, vulnerability, trust & intimacy.

Think about your favorite family memory. Maybe you sat down to watch a favorite movie together. How do those moments feel?

Now think about doing the same thing with someone you don't like. How would that experience be different? Would it be more or less enjoyable?

In which experience would you enjoy the conversation more?

When you are with the people who mean something to you, every experience improves. When you watch your favorite television show or a game with someone who's into it, it's a very different experience than watching with someone who doesn't care. Connecting makes the difference.

When you use coaching hacks, the relationship you have with that other person is powerful. **Coaching is a relational connection built on transparency, vulnerability, trust & intimacy.**

But how do you know when you are connecting with the other person (the first step in the CHAIN)? You need four things: transparency, trust, vulnerability, and intimacy.

Take a look at these working definitions:
- Transparency: Being able to present yourself exactly as you are.
- Vulnerability: Being able to listen to any feedback the other person may have for you.
- Trust: Being able to ask any question that seems important to the coach.
- Intimacy: Being confident that you can rely on the answer your client is giving you.

When these four areas are on point, the relationship is teed up for success. When even one of them is off base, the effectiveness of your conversations is at risk.

Coaching can sometimes produce a powerful feeling that I always dread. As I'm hanging up the phone at the end of a call, I take an inventory of how I'm feeling.

I look at my thoughts about the coaching session that just ended. I look at my attitude about the person with whom I'm working. I pay attention to the tension I feel in my body. I watch the progress that got made in the coaching conversation. But most of all, I pay attention to whether or not I'm looking forward to the next time I talk to this particular client.

My attitude tells me a lot.

If my outlook is right about our next conversation, it probably means that the relationship is in a stable place. But if I'm already thinking "*Wow, I'm glad that's over,* "or "*I'm thrilled to be done for this month.*" It tells me that something is wrong in the relationship. We aren't connecting.

Fortunately, adverse reactions are rare, because I work pretty hard to only coach people with whom I can have a meaningful relationship. But when less-than-stellar emotions come up, I know that I have gotten sideways with the first phase of the coaching process: Connecting.

In the Connecting phase, I'm establishing or re-establishing enough relationship so that I can ask hard questions to the people I coach. Tough questions are the only thing that matters in coaching because exploration spurs a client to new thinking.

The relationship has to be right to break new ground.

Clients often say that their coaching calls are fun. Connecting makes a call fun and useful. Excellent coaches know that coaching time should be something to which clients look forward. There's a particularly meaningful joy that makes conversations more impactful.

Using humor appropriately to connect is a high-level coaching hack. I think I'm a funny guy, but that is not something that comes up very often in a review of coaching conversations.

Humor has a place in coaching when used sparingly and appropriately. Appropriate humor can be a multiplier of the results you get in your coaching. Game theory argues that people are more likely to grow and develop new skills, and you can see that fun--and funny--have a place in coaching. But what is it?

Having the ability to laugh solidifies the relationship between client and coach. It builds trust. Humor is memorable. Great moments in life stick better with laughs. Your brain operates better when you're laughing and having fun. Humans perceive fun experiences as easier.

But when you use coaching hacks, the connection is the thing. Every word, funny or not, must move toward the client toward their goals. Every word you say has power.

Coaching starts with connecting. That's the first letter in the acronym (CHAIN) that lays out the coaching process. It does come down to how well you work with your client. It's about connection, it's about the relationship, and it's about what's possible when two people work together.

The Key Habit: Be transparent and vulnerable with people, which builds trust and intimacy.

What Now/Next: Evaluate your conversational relationships. Where do you see:
- Transparency?
- Vulnerability?
- Trust?
- Intimacy?

Key Measurements for Coaches in the Connect Phase:
- Establish/re-establish enough relationship/rapport to make coaching possible.
- Default to a generous, client-centric focus.
- Commit/Recommit to the purpose of the coaching relationship.
- Identify the client's starting point for the conversation/relationship. Connect and celebrate progress.
- Ask for/confirm opt in.

Hack: Hearing. Get the facts right.

"What we have here is a failure to communicate!" You know the movie. *Cool Hand Luke.*

Or maybe you prefer *Rush Hour,* "*Do you understand the words that are coming out of my mouth?*"

These two iconic movie lines are a coach's worst nightmare.

In an earlier hack, we explored the difference between hearing and listening. Listening is easy. You let information bounce into your brain through your ears. Hearing is another dimension entirely. Not only does the information enter your mind, but it gets processed, owned, and acted on as a result.

Those four phases in hearing are crucial. First comes input, which is another way of saying "*I receive what you are saying to me.*" get the facts right in this phase, and ensure that you're listening to what the person is saying. (This is what we most commonly call listening, but hearing goes much farther.)

Get the facts right. Then go deeper. Listen for what is beneath the surface. Always start with the facts…coaches put energy into hearing the current state the client is facing. Then we look for the changes the other person wants to make. Compelling conversations start here, and it's why the Hearing Phase lives in the first X of our simple diagram.

When you use coaching hacks, your ears become the gateway to where your client is AND where they want to be.

Next comes processing, which means taking the new data and converting it into something that you can understand and fit into your own story. Your brain fires as it integrates new input into your thought patterns. While this happens, coaches focus on the other person and integrate new thinking.

The coach owns what they're thinking about the client making sure the next question helps. When your thoughts center on the client and their situation, you have the highest likelihood of being able to ask a question that digs beneath the surface and gets to the root cause. Ownership makes you and your client capable of getting to what's causing a particular situation because you take responsibility for it.

That's what has to happen in every coaching conversation. The coach takes responsibility in asking the best questions they can come up with from what they've heard from the client.

The client assumes responsibility for exploring what's going on in their situation and themselves and acting on it appropriately. The client only works on what they learned, about themselves or the situation. The target is to make progress on things that can change based on their realizations. Hearing stands apart from listening because hearing sets up the client to take action. It all starts with ownership.

The final phase is seeing your client get into motion. Think about driving a car for a moment. When you're traveling down the road at 40 miles an hour, you only have to turn the steering wheel a slight amount to see a significant change of direction. That's one of the beautiful things about being in motion. When you're standing still or maybe backing out of a parking space, you have to turn the wheel farther to change direction. When you're in motion, you need less energy to change direction. Action makes other things easier.

A great goal for your hearing is to hold where the client is and where they want to be in your mind. It's even better if your client can grab onto those two places as well.

If the *Connecting* phase is like the foundation of the house, then *Hearing* is like the wood framing. Connecting gives you something to stand on. Hearing begins to support where you're going and might suggest the first, tentative steps in the right direction.

When you get stuck coaching, default back to listening. More questions won't help, more actions won't help. Better hearing will.

The Key Habit: Work to listen for what your client wants from the conversation. Then help them get there.

What Now/Next: Explore how you will work through the four phases of listening in your conversations. How can you use this framework in the background of your next conversation?

Key Measurements for Coaches in the Hear Phase:

- Listen for facts, emotions, motivations and the story underneath the story.
- Ask bold questions that help the client discover new insight.
- Dance a conversational dance with the client, centering on the client's agenda.
- Actively and accurately confirm what the client is saying, listening between the words if necessary.
- Establish and confirm the coaching agreement for the session/relationship.

Hack: Articulating. Helping the client NAME what they want.

Because coaching is a relationship, and relationships work primarily the same way no matter if it's coaching, a professional relationship or even a marriage, I'd like to tell you a story hits close to home. (Maybe think of this as me modeling transparency & vulnerability like we discussed a few hacks back.)

My wife and I were married just a few months. We felt (and still feel) very fortunate to have found each other since we weren't married until we were around 40 years old. After having been single my entire life to that point, my ways settled into familiar routines. Moving in with my wife and my daughter was a bit of a shock to my system. And their's.

My daughter Julia had just turned six, and she had never had a *boy in her house*. My wife Joyce loves to serve and give to people and suddenly had more people in her house. I knew waking up by myself every morning. Suddenly, I had these two beautiful girls around *every minute of every day.*

It took us a little while to figure out what worked and what didn't. We had a LOT of conversations.

I remember saying to Joyce *"It would be much easier if you just told me what you wanted because then I could do it."*

The pause as she thought about what she was going to say next was probably only a few seconds, but it seemed like a week and a half. She then very carefully said, *"But I want you to know what I want, and I don't like having to tell you all the time because it seems bossy."*

My reaction doesn't make me proud. I was frustrated. Seriously.

Say what you will about the differences between men and women, or communication styles or personality styles, the fact was that we were having a hard time communicating because we weren't saying what we wanted in a way the other person could understand.

We were at an impasse. I remember saying, "Well I can't do anything about something not on my radar." And Joy agreed, but still wanted me *just to know*. I needed to learn what my wife truly needed from me so that I could live up to her expectations. My wife needed to learn what I needed to hear from her. In the beginning, she had to lay it out step-by-step. I needed somewhat excruciating detail to get it right. She knew what she wanted, but wanted me to know her so well that I didn't need her to say it time and time again.

Our communication hit a turning point, just as in every effective coaching conversation.

Bottom line: **you typically have to SAY it before you can DO it** (or ask anyone else to do it)! When you're using coaching hacks, you help the client name what they want! The ground may shift under your client's feet, and that energy catapults them to new action!

In the CHAIN model, we call this the Articulate Moment or the *Articulating Phase*. When the light bulb comes on, the client may be coming to new realizations. Or those realizations might be familiar, but they begin to take on new meaning.

Another version of Articulating would be seemingly unrelated thoughts coalescing into action. The Articulate Moment is the outward expression of the internal connections a client makes during the Hearing Phase. The coaching relationship ramps up for action or redirects toward a new action.

Maybe it's an acknowledgment of a dream they've had.
Or a clear statement of the next steps that are staring them in the face.
Possibly a realization about who they are and they're wiring.

It could even be a complete redirect of the purpose of the coaching relationship or their life. None of those changes can happen until the client says it.

How we handle the Articulate Moment is what separates coaches from counselors, consultants, and mentors. Coaches draw the Articulate Moment out of the client.

When a breakthrough comes, it's tempting to stop. But that's the worst thing when you're using coaching hacks. Application and action close the loop.

New insights are powerful. But they quickly lose their power when they're not applied. After the lightbulb moment, a competent coach pushes for application in real life, and in real time.

The coaching question after the Articulate Moment might be "What are you going to do with this insight before we talk again?" Urgency builds due to the implication that you'll ask about it in the next conversation. If you let the client enjoy her insight but do nothing with it, you're not facilitating change. (If nothing's changing, you're not coaching!)

The uncomfortable part is that you won't necessarily know how the application happens. You might brainstorm some action steps, but the real result comes in the next coaching conversation. You have to be willing to wait for the client to move. That's not always comfortable, but it works.

The Key Habit: Watch for the Articulate Moment, when the other person can say what they want!

What Now/Next: Practice not speaking after a client has a great insight. Space for thinking further about what they're going to do encourages the client to keep digging.

Key Measurements for Coaches in the Articulate Phase:
- Draw out new realizations and insights using the client's language.
- Patiently help the client frame and reframe what they want.
- Facilitate client brainstorming.
- While dancing between generous listening and bold questions, help the client name their deepest need(s). (The Articulate Moment).
- Conduct the conversation so that the client chooses their way forward.

Hack: Implementing. Getting into action.

The first vacation I took as an adult was a bit of disaster. I had had a little success at work, and knew I needed to get away but didn't want to go through all the hassle of actually planning a trip. You know...Making hotel reservations, thinking about what I wanted to do (or not do), maybe buying a plane ticket (this was all in the pre-internet days when you had to CALL to make a reservation) ...none of that had any appeal. I just wanted to *go*.

So that's what I did. I decided just to drive and see what adventure I could find.

Walking out to my car, I wondered what I should take with me. The list had to be short (it was a small car), but I still had NO IDEA. I settled on a week of clothes, my golf clubs, and a book of maps. (Again, this was before the internet.)

I got into my car and started out with no destination in mind. No idea where I was going to sleep that night. And no idea of what I would do on my vacation. The only thing I knew for sure is that I had to be back at work a week from Monday. Everything else was up for grabs.

(By the way, this story ends with me in Branson, Missouri seeing shows with Bobby Vinton, Andy Williams and some other artists that, shall we say, had seen their heyday when my parents were young. If you've never heard of these folks, that's ok. You're making my point. Talented folks. Great entertainers. Not exactly the group I would have chosen, if I had done ANY PLANNING AT ALL.)

If I had a coach in those days, I'm sure he/she would have asked me "*What did you learn from this, ahem, adventure?*" I would probably have said something like "*Planning for a trip is annoying, but it makes the trip better.*" I might have said something like "*Next time there will be a plan, even if I not the one who makes it!*"

Steven Covey would have approved of what I realized, after the fact. What I didn't do was begin my trip with the end in mind. I knew I should have. I realized that I was the kind of person who needed to think first then act. Remember the conversation-action cycle? Conversation THEN action is the ideal order for me.

I hope you think of 25-year-old Jonathan sitting in those theaters in Branson, Missouri in your next coaching conversation. My experience illustrates the power of the Implementing Phase.

Remember the illustration of the CHAIN:

Figure 6 -- Remember the CHAIN Model?

In the Implementing Phase, we've moved our focus to the second X, and now our client is making progress toward what they want to accomplish and how they want to get it done.

The goal in the Implementing Phase is always to move you closer to that second X. It might be a small step or a big one. There might not be measurable progress at all. A lack of distance traveled can be helpful if you are learning because of the effort.

My first boss, way back in my radio career days, used to say, *"Plan your work then work your plan."* Application of the Implementing Phase starts here.

When you're using coaching hacks, your posture is to help the client name where they are and where they want to be. Building on the Articulate Moment coaches in the Implementing Phase assist the client making sound decisions about where they are going to go and how they are going to get there.

BTW...The order in the CHAIN model matters. Without connecting, you can't hear what your client is saying. Without hearing, you won't know when they've articulated. Without articulating, you won't have any confidence that your client is implementing the correct plan. Articulating always comes before implementing. No way around it.

If you implement first and THEN articulate what you want, your client is at risk. Coaches that help their clients get at risk don't have clients for very long. Risk leads to the classic ready, fire, aim!

After a breakthrough moment, or an articulate moment, our human tendency is to get going implementing which sometimes pushes 25-year-old single guys to vacation in Branson, Missouri (not that there's anything wrong with that). But it's often much more helpful to pause long enough to think about what will get me where I want to go next.

Coaches who can help their clients choose a significant action after an Articulate Moment change lives. No formula exists for this. You can think your way into a new way of acting. Or you can act your way into a new way of thinking. What matters is the action that gets you where you want to go. **Planning for change needs both new thinking and new action. Either can come first.**

Using coaching hacks at a high-level means putting energy into both "What will I do next?" AND "How does this help me get where I want to go?" In the coaching world, we would refer to this as working with Plans and Actions.

Here are some working definitions:

Plans are what gets done over the life of the coaching relationship. Every client has to make their plans, and effective coaches listen well, ask questions that draw out new insight and wisdom, and help the client commit to a course of action. Think of plans as the big picture thrusts of what has to happen for the client to accomplish what they want. Plans can be unseen strategies that the client executes to get where they want to go.

All of this happens before a client does anything.

Actions are what's going on in between coaching conversations. A real action gets the other person into motion. Effective coaches help their clients evaluate whether the measures they want to take will move them towards their goals and their purpose. If they do, it's probably a good choice. Actions are the visible and tactical evidence that the client is getting into motion.

Plans and actions are made stronger by a clear sense of purpose. Why is this important to your client? And why have they come to you for help?

Note: the more detailed your ending vision is, the easier it is to lay out steps along the way. Spending time assessing the starting point makes a difference, but the best possible investment in plans and actions is a clear vision of where you want to end up.

That vision might change during your coaching relationship. That's fine, but as a coach, it's your responsibility to ensure that the client doesn't do that lightly. What does your client want? Implement toward that!

The Key Habit: Immediately after an Articulate Moment, ask the other person *"What action will get you where you want to go?"*

What Now/Next: Learn to distinguish between what has to happen in the life span of a relationship and what needs to happen before the next conversation.

Key Measurements for Coaches in the Implement Phase:
- Finalize the choice of action step, building on client forward motion.
- Ensure the action plan moves the client toward big picture goals.
- Develop action steps.
- Explore accountability systems.
- Confirm the timeline.

Hack: Noticing. What's the difference because of this conversation?

Your brain never shuts off, even when asleep. One of the brain's prime functions is to catalog what is different now compared to the last time the brain went over a particular thought pattern or mental map.

Brain wiring is equipped to make a note of what is different. We can't help it, and it's what our brains are designed to do. When you use coaching hacks, you naturally take advantage of this pattern.

Near the end of one recent coaching session, I asked: "What has changed for you since we started coaching together?"

David had to think about it for a while. But then he came up with a long list of things he learned about himself and realizations he had come to about his leadership. He now could name what pushed his buttons, and situations where he was especially effective. After three or four minutes of listing off things he commented: "I guess I'm looking at my situation completely differently, even though my circumstances don't seem to have changed very much."

The last phase in the CHAIN model is Noticing.

Noticing is the both the easiest and the hardest step in the process. On the one hand, it's easy just to see what your client is accomplishing, but on the contrary, there will be plenty of times where progress is almost imperceptible. That's why it's more powerful to help the client notice their progress. When you use coaching hacks, your role is to help the other person make progress of their choosing. Sometimes you won't be able to see it, but they will.

Have you ever been to a bar or restaurant where they have one of those video games that features side-by-side images? When you play the game, you find the difference—and sometimes those differences are subtle. Usually the same photo is used, but with a few alterations to make sure that you're paying attention.

The Noticing Phase works this way, using side-by-side comparison.

Think about that game in your mind as a coach in the Noticing Phase. The first image represents where the client begins a conversation. The more clearly you understand and can remember what that beginning point is like, the better.

The finishing place is the second image. Your job as a coach is to draw out of the client what differences they want to see in that second picture.

A side-by-side comparison is a great tool. The Noticing Phase is an intentional choice, requiring you to take stock of where you started and the progress you've made. **Pay attention to what's different because of this conversation/relationship.** Especially what's different through the client's eyes.

The Noticing Phase leads to celebration. It feels good when your client's face shows they know they are making progress toward their vision! The coach should celebrate that as well.

David was a great example. Sometimes a client notices visible results to be checked off the to do list. Other times internal growth sets the stage for extraordinary results that will come later. Both of these are effective forms of noticing. Always invite the other person to see how far they've come.

But some wise coach is reading this and saying *"Which one is better internal noticing or external?"*

The answer is yes. It depends on both the client and the situation. Masterful coaches only notice where the client makes progress. You, the coach, don't get to predetermine what they're going to see. The client might decide where they want to end up, but you must have the coaching conversation and implement the plan that your client makes.

When you're using coaching hacks to notice a change, you can frame the discussion in at least two ways: Units and Deltas.
- Units: Exactly what is changing during the coaching process.
- Delta: How MUCH change you see during the coaching process.

Both of these measurements can be helpful. Knowing what will change gives you focus on asking better questions. Knowing how much will change sets expectations and builds trust.

Noticing often happens in the background of a coaching conversation. It does make sense to look for results first, as a primary orientation. It's just easier to see visible results than internal growth. One of the most significant coaching hacks of all is "don't make it harder than it has to be." If your client is getting something done, celebrate!

But if your client is struggling to see visible results, a best practice for coaching hacks is to invite the other person to turn the conversation internal. They will confirm what they're learning about themselves, or where their emotional or spiritual life is playing out, or even how their perception of the situation has changed.

The results matter. A tricky thing about coaching: you can use all of the high-quality coaching techniques the world, but if your clients don't see effective results you have failed.

The Key Habit: Draw out of personal insights into how your client makes progress.

What Now/Next: Game plan for your next conversation around the Units (What will be changing?) and the Delta (How much change will they see?).

Key Measurements for Coaches in the Notice Phase:
- Discover points for celebration.
- Mark progress from the beginning (of the session and the relationship).
- Help the client name the change (and the connected emotions) they are experiencing.
- Connect current conversation with next outcomes.
- Confirm next conversation.

Hack: Shift Happens.

Every spring, a moment comes when you're sure that winter is over. You move into spring mode. There's another one just like it when spring becomes to summer.

The world around us changes at that moment. If you live in the North as I do, the driveway looks different because you won't be getting the snow blower out again. The lawn looks different because soon you'll be pushing the mower. That shift changes everything.

And it's the same moment that makes coaching so effective.

When you're using coaching hacks, your conversations facilitate moments like this. Without any warning, the other person begins to see their world differently. Coaching magic starts here. The shift happens when suddenly the client's perspective changes or they see things that they couldn't see before.

Shift happens. Get ready for it!

You can't predict the shift. The relationship has to be on the right track, with high levels of trust and client-coach intimacy. The purpose of the relationship is crystal clear. And the coach is doing everything a coach can do to offer a high-quality, high commitment coaching presence.

But even when all of these things are happening, there's no guarantee the client will experience a shift. But when shift happens, your client is boldly going where they've never gone before. There's nothing you can do to stop them. In fact, you won't want to stop there. Please don't!

Usually the client will tell you when the shift happens. It's noisy! You might hear an exclamation *"Wow! I just realized something!"* or *"I just had a thought I've never had before."* Or *"Well, this changes everything!"* (Like coaching does!)

Simply put, the Shift is an internal change that has external applications and implications.

Imagine a client that leads a medium-to-large organization. In a coaching conversation, the topic of staff reductions comes up. That's an uncomfortable question in any circumstance. The client says "*People's lives are going to be changed by this.*"

The coach might ask "*In what ways?*" or "*How do you see these effects playing out?*" A better question would be "*What's at stake for you?*" That is inviting the client to think about the internal shifts THEY would have to make.

What would you do if the client responded to what's at stake with "*I consider all these people my friends, and I don't want to fire my friends.*" As soon as those words are out of the other person's mouth, their world is different.

Shift happens. At least we hope it does.

When you're using coaching hacks, what you do next is counter-intuitive. Be quiet. Let the client come to terms with how they've just shifted. The world appears differently now than moments earlier. Give them space.

Masterful coaching is the ability draw out of the client key insights & observations that will help the client shift their perspective(s) to a new, healthier place. The best coaches do this all the time, and probably don't even think about it. The rest of us have to learn to react this way.

The Shift is powerful. And good things come quickly right afterward. Once your perspective changes, actions and plans get easier to design and accomplish. The Shift is something about which to be excited! It's time to celebrate!

Some of my best coaching moments have come when all I say is "That sounded significant." That's it. The client will pick it up from there. Remember, silence is your friend. Listen 80%. Talk 20%

Once the client has a chance to process the Shift, then it's time to ask for action. "What will you do now?" is a good approach. Or "What is different as a result of what you've realized?"

The Shift is addictive. Nothing moves a coaching relationship forward like The Shift. When you're using coaching hacks, Shift Happens.

The Key Habit: Learn to sense the Shift when it happens to the person you're talking with and give them space to continue to build on it.

What Now/Next: Make a list of situations where you would rather point out something than draw something out of another person.

Hack: Focus on root causes, NOT presenting symptoms.

This particular client and I had been circling an issue for 40 minutes or so. I was doing my best, asking open ended questions and inviting him to say more. He was stuck. The rut was getting deeper with every question. Finally, he said, *"Why don't you tell me what you see?"*

Every coach has been in this situation. The client has asked for your opinion--you probably have one--and permitted you to express it. The effectiveness of this coaching session hangs in the balance. What's a coach to do?

When you're using coaching hacks, you go right at the situation, through the side door: Ask the client what's holding them back, in some level of bluntness, and offer something to see what picks up. In this particular case, I said: *"I see a guy who's stuck. What are you avoiding that is keeping you stuck?"*

It was bold and risky. Without knowing for sure, my intuition was my guide.

The client didn't say anything for a long time. Then he stammered, *"Well, there is one issue that I haven't wanted to bring up..."*

He then unpacked an item that, on the surface, seemed only loosely related to what on which we were working. But the longer he talked, the more directly connected it became. The hesitation was because we found a critical issue that he had caused.

Before too long, he saw a different way forward. He had a significant shift in what he was expecting from himself and his situation.

The lesson we can learn from this story is that often the Presenting Symptom is different that the Key Issue. **Focus on root causes, not presenting symptoms.**

The Presenting Symptom is what appears to be going on. It's the thing that demands the majority of the time in the early phases of the coaching relationship. We can easily get caught up in the presenting symptom and miss the thing that will help our clients change. The presenting symptom is valuable to understand because it often points to the root cause of the situation (which leads to the solution).

The Key Issue is what needs to be addressed to facilitate a lasting and meaningful change in a particular situation. It's not always easy to see, but working on it always leads to a significant shift, even if you have to take more than one pass at it.

Think of the Key Issue as what's going on in a situation. Here's a metaphor I like:

Picture a beautiful, calm morning next to the ocean. You're walking along the beach, and the water is still. The surface of the water is the presenting symptom. It seems calm and tranquil. Like there's nothing but good things going on. (Often this is what the initial conversations of a coaching relationship are like.)

But then a scuba diver walks down the beach and dives into the water. What do you think they're seeing? Underwater life, the coral reef, plants, fish, maybe a shipwreck and even the occasional shark or another marine predator! With this perspective, where could you work? What conversation could you have? Picking out an area to focus your efforts on that can make a difference is MUCH easier and more efficient when you have this perspective under the surface.

The ICF coaching competency of *Powerful Questioning* is what it takes to get beneath the surface. When you're using coaching hacks, every conversation centers on the fundamental question: *what's going on?* The answer requires us to be honest with ourselves.

Why do we hesitate to be straight with ourselves? Our hesitance is the single biggest reason why coaching relationships don't get to the heart of the issue. Effective coaches partner with their clients to overcome that hesitation and dig through the layers of the story to what's going on.

The Key Habit: Don't get caught up coaching the symptoms of a situation. The Key Issue is always about the other person and needs attention. Lasting change grows from here.

What Now/Next: Think about times when you have been caught up in symptoms in some situation you were facing. How did you get through it? How could you apply this approach in a conversation with someone else?

Hack: Coaching starts BEFORE the conversation.

Quick review: who should be the hero of every coaching conversation? The client should. If you take nothing else from this book, embrace that. This *one hack binds them all* and makes all the other hacks more effective, and it will change every conversation you have. See Coaches make the client the hero.

It's not all up to you though. Someone else joins you in the conversation, every time. The other half of the conversation has some work to do. Your client is heroic, after all!

When you're using coaching hacks, clear expectations for what it takes to be in a conversation with you multiplies your potential effect. Some of the expectations are yours, and some have to be owned by the client. In truth, **coaching starts BEFORE the conversation** for both coach and client.

Coaching sports helps our paradigm here. No coach who wants to stay employed plays without a game plan. She knows which players are going to play, the other team's weaknesses, the matchups she wants, and how she'll adjust if her plan doesn't work. She doesn't know all the details, but she knows how she's going to start.

Before a coaching session, have a game plan for coaching. Get yourself into the proper frame of mind. Turn off your cell phone, or mute all the notifications. Review your notes from the last session. Get rid of distractions. Make sure you don't have drama going on that might spill over into the session. I even like to pick out my first question ahead of time. Usually it's something like "What's going well in your world right now?" so that we start on an upbeat note.

Clients can prepare as well. At the very least, ask the other person to have a focus for your coaching conversations in mind BEFORE you start. Before a meaningful conversation, it might help to send an email with a couple of items that will prepare your client to show up ready to work.

Here are some sample questions:
- What are the three things you're celebrating now?
- What are three changes you know you need to make?
- What are the 1 or 2 things you want to take away from this conversation?
- What is your biggest challenge right now?

- What do you want to work on in this session?
- What key issues/ideas do you need to explore?

Any forward momentum the client has when you start will make you more effective!

The Key Habit: Get your ducks in a row before each coaching session.

What Now/Next: Examine what would make you most effective in your ongoing conversations.

Hack: <mark>You can't work on what's</mark> already happened.

My client and I collaborated on this project for six months. For close to a dozen sessions, the topic was a giant launch of a new product. My client invested in making a big splash.

Our last session was about a week before the launch. The next few weeks were going to be busy for my client, and hard for me waiting to hear how it went. Finally, our next session came.

"What's been going on for you?" I asked at the session start. The client ran through a list of personal and professional breakthroughs but didn't mention the launch.

"You seem like you're in a good place. What do you want to work on in this session?" was my next comment and question.

The client brought up a new topic, and we got to work. Near the end of the session, I asked about the launch.

"I was hoping that wouldn't come up. We almost made it to the end of the session," he said. I couldn't believe my ears.

"What happened?" Three days before the launch, a day or two after our last session, the project was pulled. I think I was more disappointed than my client. I immediately went to a dark place, wondering why my client didn't think to call me and tell me.

A laundry list of factors played into the decision, and as my client described them, he was completely calm. Maybe even GOOD WITH THE DECISION! That was pretty different than how I was feeling!

My client had come to terms with the decision and admitted that he had second guessed his leadership for a while. Eventually, he moved on. He somehow knew **you couldn't work on what's already happened.**

The pastor Charles Swindoll says *"Life is 10% what happens to you and 90% how you react to it."*[7] My client understood this. There was nothing he could do, as the decision was made higher up the food chain than where he had influence.

The coaching equivalent of this might be coaching topics are 10% what happened to your client, and 90% how they respond in the session. A genuine measure of a coach is not what happens to your client, but how you draw out their response.

When you're using coaching hacks, the current circumstances set the stage for future growth. My client realized that his time could be better used working on the next initiative. He leveraged our coaching time to work toward new goals. It was a very healthy and appropriate reaction.

(Over the next nine months or so, my client got into conversations with his employer about the canceled project, and eventually resurrected parts of it. He led the new initiative and ended up getting promoted. His reaction in the immediate aftermath was a key component in this promotion.)

The Key Habit: Focus your conversational time and energy on current critical issues in which you can have an impact.

What Now/Next: Learn to tailor all your questions so that your client can move forward, despite what has happened to them recently.

Hack: Conflict has power. Use it.

There is a moment in a jazz composition where the tension rises. It can be just about unbearable...in an excellent way. For a few measures, the notes don't seem to work. They just don't fit together. Sometimes it gets to the point where *it just doesn't seem right.*

The soloist steps up and begins to play. The tension builds.

The band rises around the soloist.

Technique is at the highest level and is on full display. The synchronization of the musicians is almost like they're sharing one heart, one mind, one body or even *one soul*.

Each breath heightens the tension. Each downbeat pushes the music forward. Each musician offers what he or she has to something bigger than himself.

Everything that every player has becomes a part of the music.

And then, *it happens.*

The soloist and the band move the piece to a new level. The soloist explodes, seeing new things and offering new sounds. All of a sudden everything fits together again. Now this. *This is music!*

For the listener, this is when the experience goes to an entirely new place. The music begins to fit together in a whole new way.

And it wouldn't have worked without the tension. At least not nearly as well. For coaches, this is instructive.

You've all heard someone offer an opinion and say, "*Well, that and 4-6 dollars will get you a cup of coffee.*" My depression-era parents used to talk about adding a nickel to an opinion, but hey, times have changed. Stuff costs more.

A statement like this is often intended to be self-deprecating. I get the use of humor in a comment like this; it releases tension. We make a joke because we're a little bit uncomfortable. But stress is very helpful. **Conflict & tension have power. Use it.**

Three common scenarios cause this tension for a coach.

The cost for the person being coached has to be real. Coaching is one of the most efficient ways to help someone change. Effective coaches don't shy away from the fact that the client will have to put something at risk to get what they want. The moment when that sets in can be a little tense, but the cost is worth it. A bit of self-deprecating humor can help if it builds commitment for the client. If that moment is a distraction, then, it's probably not worth it. Learning to assess the value of a break in the tension at the moment is a high-level coaching skill that speaks to the coach's self-awareness.

Tension rises when the coach is on the verge of offering some input or feedback of their own. You might be about to bottom line the client. Or you see a chance to throw out some of your experience. Is it worth it, to step out of the formal coach role? We want to offer our opinions, but for whatever reason, we're sensitive to forcing those views on others. That's a good thing.

Something much deeper is also going on. We tend to mitigate the risk of putting our thoughts, opinions, or values out there. The only time this is real is when our own experience is helpful for the client. Always, always, always remember that we can offer some of our own experience, but it's the client's choice whether to accept it and what to do with it.

Tension JUMPS up when the financial cost of the coaching relationship becomes apparent. Every coach who's any good has a moment of hesitation when the price discussion happens. Jokes seem like a great tension-breaker. But do you believe that what you offer is worth it? If not, you should lower your prices! If you do, fight the urge to joke right then. FIGHT IT! The client is in for a battle. Change is hard. If you don't believe you can help (and that the fight, with all of its connected costs) will be worth it, YOU have more hard questions to answer than the client does.

A little tension is helpful...it makes us better as coaches and helps us stay fully present in the relationship. But too much anxiety about the worth of what you're offering is a nail in the coffin of your coaching career. After all, pressure is what makes diamonds.

The Key Habit: Let the tension sit a little longer than is naturally comfortable.

What Now/Next: Do things that cause your anxiety level to rise so that you build capacity for coaching moments.

Hack: Work for both growth and results. In that order.

My client wanted to write a book. She had been a close observer of a crucial time in America's history and wanted to be sure that her family knew about what she had seen, felt and done.

The book was going to be private. In fact, publishing the book was not an option. The story was getting written down so my client's grandchildren would know how close she had been to stories they were learning about in school. Her personal story connected to some of the great American stories.

Amazing doesn't begin to describe what she talked about in those 17 sessions. (We contracted for 12, but I couldn't walk away from her.). Near the end, I asked her made her proud from our time together.

She described how much she had learned about herself. I expected her to talk about how proud of what she had done, and what she had written down. But instead she discussed how pleased she was that she had lived according to her faith, and how well she did as a writer. Yes, the story got down on paper, but how much she had grown was the biggest win.

She was 86 when we worked together. And she never stopped growing. That is impressive.

She taught me about evaluating my coaching. Before working with Hattie, all my coaching was measured by the results it generated. But she showed me that the growth a coaching conversation produces is every bit as important. And MAYBE even more crucial.

You could map these two growth opportunities on a quadrant graph, and that will give you a clear picture of what a coaching conversation can accomplish. When you use coaching hacks, both growth and results are on the table. How would your coaching conversations land on this axis? **Work for both growth and results. In that order.**

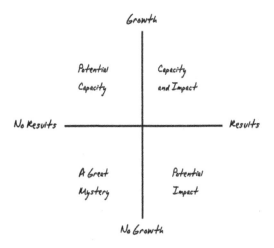

Figure 7 -- Map Out Results & Growth

Coaching for growth is about input. If you aim for results, you might get growth. Growth is dealing with what's on the inside (most of the time). Growth addresses the critical issue but doesn't necessarily facilitate any changes.

Coaching for results is about output. If you aim for growth, you almost always have results. Results are dealing with what's on the outside (most of the time). Results typically lead to treating the presenting symptom. SOMETHING will change when you coach for results, and your client has to decide if they want the change.

When you use coaching hacks, both growth and results are necessary to address the real problem sustainably.

You might think of this paradigm as including both a strategic and tactical view.

Strategy comes into play when you're aligning the actions that your client designs with the purpose of the coaching relationship. Use strategy to figure out how the big rocks line up, so the client makes much progress as possible.

Tactics come into play when the client is designing individual action steps to move them closer to the overall vision. You'll spend some time in every coaching conversation talking tactics. The best tactics line up with your stated goals and provide forward momentum that moves you closer.

The Key Habit: Invite the other person to describe what they're learning or how they're changing.

What Now/Next: The results you generate tie to your specialty or niche. About what do people typically talk to you?

Hack: Coach the person. Consult the problem. Mentor the experience. Counsel the fallout.   -

I'm a recovering consultant. Maybe you are too. Experts make a lot of money for giving people their opinion about a situation or a circumstance. That's what I love to do. I appreciate, even welcome, the opportunity to tell another person what I think.

But that's not what coaches do. Coaches help people make sense of their world and take action. Who's doing the work? The client. NOT the coach. Using coaching hacks makes it all about the person you're talking with, and only that person.

That's why the key orientation for coaching is to focus on the person with whom you're working. It's certainly not one-size-fits-all or following a pre-programmed agenda. (Any coach that wants to tell you that every one of their clients follows a particular 12 step session map is not a coach. They might be using some coaching skills, but they're not a coach.)

Coaches help clients discover what is inside of them and how to use those discoveries for ideal benefit. One coach I know tells of a client who had been a high-level executive assistant throughout her career. She had an opportunity to join the board of a very effective not-for-profit organization. As the coaching conversation played out, the client realized that she had absolutely everything required to do the job. She was equipped and ready to go. (She went on to make a great contribution to that organization through her service to the board.)

Your role as a coach is to help someone else make sense of their world and to take action on it.

Coaching is personal. No two coaching clients are the same nor are any two coaching conversations. Every single conversation is unique to the person being coached and the context that person is facing.

You're not there to teach or tell someone what they should think or do. You're there to draw out of your client what they've already got to work with...whether they know it or not.

When you're using coaching hacks, it's tempting to mistake coaching for other kinds of intentional relationships, like mentoring, counseling or consulting. It's a tricky wrinkle. Here are some guidelines:

- Counseling is about self-understanding, healing, and wholeness. There may be a diagnosis involved.
- Expert consultants specialize in diagnosing and prescribing action plans. An expert's thoughts are what they get paid to offer.
- Mentoring requires something to teach or pass on connected to a particular skill set or experience. The mentor has usually done what the client wants to do.

All the intentional relationship styles use the same skills: generous & active listening, bold & powerful questions and intentionally designed actions. The reasons behind when to do what vary a bit, and so does how the actions end up getting chosen. Let the similarity of these four styles sit with you for a minute. Choose what NOT to do just like you choose what to do.

A simple way to keep the boundaries clear is to picture the four options on a quadrant graph, like what you see below.

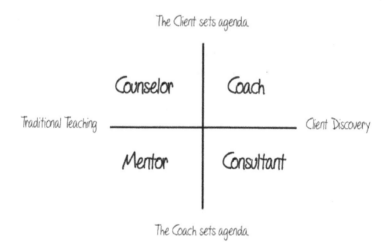

Figure 8 -- Four Types of Intentional Relationship

When you're using coaching hacks, you can move between the four quadrants, even inside of a single conversation. How do I know which quadrant I'm in at any given moment? Ask yourself two key questions:

- Who is setting the agenda for this part of the conversation? (Coaches want the client to drive.)

- How much teaching do I have to do right now? (Coaches want to draw out, not pour in.)

With a little practice, you learn to identify what your clients need at any given time and to seamlessly move to the quadrant that will serve your client most effectively.

The Key Habit: Put your energy and effort into coaching the person, NOT solving the problem or passing on your experience.

What Now/Next: Brainstorm a plan for how you're going to help your clients talk about what's most important to them, whether or not it's the same topic you think they should explore.

Hack: Ask in. Question out.

Your experience in life and coaching will naturally draw people to you. Everyone is looking for someone who has done what they want to do. The input of someone who has been there informs significant decisions.

But if the client always gets to choose and if they're the hero of every coaching situation, how do you handle those moments when your client just wants you to tell them what you would do in a particular moment?

My ideal client is a leader who is starting something, maybe a new business, or a church or a new initiative in their company. In my previous career, starting new television shows or launching new radio stations was a big part of my experience. I tend to always look for a new way to do something, rather than repeat what someone else has done.

My wiring is both an asset to my coaching and a burden. Using my natural tendencies to benefit the client is tricky sometimes. After all, I'm a recovering consultant.

Ashley and I were in a coaching relationship. She led change initiatives for her company and was working on a complicated team building opportunity. Budget concerns, cultural differences on this international project, change overload, and an aggressive marketing campaign were all factors she was managing. Her situation reminded me of one of my former TV stations developed new programming.

We went around and around about all the various details. I had something I wanted to say but sensed that it might distract from the momentum. My instinct was the plan needed a few small re-directs.

When you use coaching hacks, you can offer your input but ONLY if the client permits you. After you do, the client gets to decide what to do with your contribution.

I wanted to consult Ashley, to give her my assessment of her situation. I even had a couple of actions I thought she should consider. But I didn't have permission.

So I asked for it. *"Would it be all right if I threw a couple of things out to you?"*

She paused and said *"In a minute. I need to think this through first."*

What a great response! She knew she was making progress and didn't want to get side tracked. She continued to process her thinking out loud.

After a few minutes, she asked for my input. I gave it, and quickly added: "*What is coming to mind now?*" She jumped right in and picked up her processing. By the end of the conversation, she had made a detailed plan (and some decisions about what I had offered).

Moments like this illustrate a fundamental behavior for when you're using coaching hacks: **Ask in to one of the other quadrants. And question your way out.** Ashley permitted me to move into the consultant quadrant, and she valued my input. In this case she didn't decide to act on what I had to say, but she included it in her thinking.

My key choice was NOT to make a case for why my way was the best way. Offering my options was enough. Immediately I went back to my coaching posture and got out of her way as she made her choices.

When using coaching hacks, the goal is to equip the other person with the benefits of your experience. But always let them choose what to do with it.

The Key Habit: Remember that your experience matters, but the client's choices matter even more.

What Now/Next: Write down a strategy for how you will get in and out of those moments when your experience looms large in the client's eyes.

Hack: You can only coach as far as your client will let you.

My mentor coach was trying to be nice. We were reviewing a recording of a recent coaching session I had with Diane, one of my clients. *"You asked a lot of compelling questions,"* he said several times. *"What did you learn from them?"*

"Not much," I said.

"What does that tell you?" he continued.

I thought long and hard. *"I'm not sure my questions were that bold or powerful. At least, they didn't discover anything."*

"What got in your way?"

We went around and round like this. My mentor coach told me about how well I'd structured my questions, and how seriously he thought my client had taken them. I kept claiming it didn't take us anywhere. Finally, I had a breakthrough.

"My client got in the way! No matter what I asked, she didn't want to answer!" I was exasperated.

"Exactly. Sometimes, no matter what you do, your client just doesn't want to go there. So what will you do differently next time?"

That day I learned a valuable lesson. We were working on a core idea tied to the purpose of the coaching relationship, but for some reason, my client wasn't ready to go there. It happens. Coaches, by our very nature, want good things for our clients. It's a part of who we are, and why we became coaches in the first place. When the client isn't ready, it sets a ceiling on how far you can rise in a particular coaching conversation. There is not much we can do about it.

Remember the simple framework for every coaching conversation:
- Take a snapshot of where you are.
- Develop a vision of where you want to be.
- Shorten the distance.

In the purest sense, using coaching hacks means your role is to be content neutral, non-directional. You don't add any of your expectations or skills. You come alongside the other person, and help them figure out where they want to go. The alongside component is key. I'd even say peer-to-peer learning trumps teacher/instructor-student conversation.

If the client doesn't want to go, using coaching hacks won't take you anywhere helpful. (You might run LOTS of unhelpful places!) Your role is to coach, to draw out. If the client resists, stop coaching.

If you see this situation regularly in your coaching (in one or more relationships), you will likely need to re-define what you're doing. Something is off track. You might have slipped out of the kind of relationship a coach has. Or the purpose may have become unclear. Or you may not be integrating coaching hacks as seamlessly as your client needs.

Even if what you're doing requires reinvention, you can still use coaching hacks to make a measurable and observable impact in every conversation.

The Key Habit: Learning to stop and re-focus a coaching conversation means leaning into what gives coaching hacks power.

What Now/Next: Use a simple Intake/onboard/impact evaluation tool to set your relationships up for success.
- Intake means to determine if you can develop enough relationship to coach the person and identify the purpose of the coaching.
- Onboard means find some early wins in the coaching, so your client gains trust and momentum.
- Impact means keeping your eyes on why the person came to you in the first place and how you'll measure effectiveness.

Hack: Being generous wins.

A former client sent me an email a while ago. He commented that he was reaping the benefits of the work we did together, even after a couple of years.

This coaching relationship did not go the way I thought it should or would. A lot of energy went into trying to help him decide what he wanted, and we did some deep character work (root cause, not presenting symptom) about who he is and where he's going.

When I hung up from those calls, my thoughts ran to "I sure hope this is working for him, because I'm exhausted." My client never actually said anything either way, but I noticed he didn't renew our coaching relationship when it ended.

Sometimes I felt like the whole relationship was a failure. Two years later, I could see that it wasn't.

The lesson here is that it's not about you. Or at least it shouldn't be.

What would your world be like if you consistently chose to make it about the other person?

Being generous wins. Every time. Be generous. That means leveraging the gifts, talents, experience, and knowledge you've got not only to make your own life better but to make the world better for other people. Remember that's the definition of coaching.

Here's why being generous matters: you can be giving and have it still be all about you. When you are generous, it can't be about you at all.

When you use coaching hacks, you tap into an unique drive that other people don't have: we are as much about other people's growth and development as we are about our own. Maybe we're even more about how others develop.

The point of a coaching relationship is to ensure that the person you're working with gets where they want to go, and receives all the good stuff that comes with it.

You can choose to be in a generous posture. It's like changing your shirt. You take off the old "me agenda" and put on the new "you agenda."

I dream of a world where people start conversations with questions about the other person and not with statements about themselves.

Some of who you are will rub off on your client. That's a basic rule of relationships. So, little by little, you're developing the people around you by inviting them to not be all about themselves, and simultaneously be about US. The world needs more of this. The best of you gets offered to the best of them, and both of you are better off.

You can't help it. A little bit of who you rubs off on everyone with whom you connect. When you use coaching hacks, you're intentionally saying "I have something to offer you, and it's yours if you want it."

If you are uncomfortable reproducing who you are then maybe you should work on yourself.

The Key Habit: Put on a generous shirt every morning.

What Now/Next: Learn how to tell when you've got the "Me Shirt" on and when you've changed to the "You Shirt" or the "Us Shirt."

Hack: No two coaches are the same.

Chris became a long-time client. That's how the story ended.

My friend Tim is a terrific coach. He listens by default, asks great questions, and draws actions out of his clients. He began coaching Chris after another coach retired and found new coaches for his continuing clients. The relationship didn't start well.

Chris had specific expectations about how the coaching relationship would go, based on his experience with his first coach. But Tim had a different style, vocabulary and even pace to his coaching. Together they struggled to generate the same growth and results that Chris expected.

At the core, these two guys were about all the same things. They had similar values, experience, and priorities. Tim was committed to being an asset for Chris' development. But it wasn't working.

After 5 or 6 sessions, Tim decided to speak up. Chris confirmed his suspicions and admitted his concern about the relationship. It was an ah-ha moment for Tim. They had no connection, other than the couple hours they spent together coaching.

They had the advantage of living in the same town, so they scheduled a coffee appointment. Business was off the table in this conversation; this was just about learning about the other person. They discovered that they had kids about the same age. They both followed the local football team and had seats to the games a couple of sections apart. They knew some people in common. They even had similar senses of humor.

The next coaching session was entirely different. A working foundation and a little bit of shared history connected them. Tim and Chris could now see each other as people, and not just as coach and client. A few sessions later, Chris was seeing the best development in the entire time he had had a coach. Tim was his guy!

In an evaluation conversation at the end of their first coaching contract, Chris commented that Tim was very different from his first coach. Chris continued about his pleasant surprise at how well that worked for him. It's true. **No two coaches are the same.** And no two coaches can generate the same results, even with the same client.

When you use coaching hacks, how you are in your relationships is how you are in your coaching relationships. It's important to remember that you bring your entire self into every conversation.

Using coaching hacks means finding your coaching voice. And sticking with it. You won't be able to use the same questions or strategies in the same way as anyone else. Learn from others, but put your mark on how they do things.

My mentor Bob Logan used to ask a precise question in a lot of his coaching conversations "How can we increase the learning in this situation?" I LOVED that question. But whenever I would try to use it, it landed flat. That's not how I talk. It's perfect for Bob but doesn't work for me. At all.

"What else can we learn from this?" is the same question. But that's MY coaching voice. I would say that in lots of situations, not just coaching.

When I have a foundation of relationship with my client, I'm free to be who I am and so is the client. Even if we don't agree on everything, we have enough between us so that we can transparently and authentically get at what matters.

A cheesy way to remember this is that coaches are like snowflakes. No two are exactly alike!

The Key Habit: Invest a little time in building relational capital with you client.

What Now/Next: Make a short list of your key coaching values, so that you are crystal clear on who you are and how you come across to your client.

Hack: Speak the truth, but leave the meaning & interpretation alone.

Remember <u>the conversation with Dominic?</u> He was working to find a focus for our conversation, and I was simultaneously questioning whether I should ever coach again.

It was dangerous for coach Jonathan. My self-talk ALMOST got the better of me. My active mind took me to a risky place. The fight or flight response was on the verge of taking over. The relationship with Dominic was in definite danger that day.

When you use coaching hacks, two conversations run simultaneously: the external conversation with the client and the internal conversation with yourself. Ideally, they work together, but they do get out of sync. Masterful coaches know that self-talk affects external talk. You can learn to use your self-talk to the benefit the client. That's a prime example of using *everything* available to you to serve someone else.

The temptation is to treat this as a transaction. You get to coach, and in return, the client gets to make progress toward their goals. But the balance between internal and external conversations is more precarious.

All of us have a history, which is the main story of our lives. If we're committed to serving the client with everything we have, that means our inner monologues have a place in the conversation. **Speak the truth, but leave the meaning & interpretation alone.**

When you have thoughts that pop into your mind, speak so the other person can consider. But let them decide what to do with it. If you're skilled at this approach, you'll even let the client find the meaning of what you have to say. It might not mean the same thing to them. You're there to make them better, right?

I can think of coaching conversations where I've tossed out thoughts that seemed completely random, only to have the client say *"Wow, I can't believe that just came out of your mouth. I was just thinking..."* and then they went on to have a huge breakthrough!

The danger zone is becoming attached to having your client do something from your intuition. That's not okay. Put it out there, and see what happens.

Trust your intuition. You never know where it might take you!

The Key Habit: Listen to your inner voice. Intuition is powerful.

What Now/Next: Practice making observations, but let the client choose what to do. Ensure that you have permission before you put it out there.

Hack: If it's not a little scary, it might not be worth doing.

What do you do when you're scared? Or when you have a knot of fear winding up in your stomach? Millions of dollars are exchanged every month between people who are afraid of something and their counselors. These conversations are so familiar we can all picture them in our heads, or at least the movie scenes about similar discussions.

At the core of the majority of coaching conversations looms fear. The most powerful Articulate Moments are when the client names their fear for the first time. You can feel relief that when the weight lifts.

When you use coaching hacks, naming our fears focuses on immediate concerns. Coaches don't deal with the past event that started the fear cycle, but rather the future actions that will manage the fear or make that fear an asset.

People like to be afraid. The popularity of horror movies proves that. Some part of our humanity *wants* to be unnerved by what's going on in us or around us. That's a crucial distinction. Another distinction is between helpful fear (that keeps us safe or motivates us to change) and unhelpful fear (that paralyzes us or puts us at risk). One is coachable; one is not.

Dealing with scary items around us is a management technique. Coaching hacks can certainly help a client figure out how to keep what's scaring them in check.

Working on what is scary inside of us is a growth technique. Transparent and vulnerable relationships make naming your fear easier. When we acknowledge our fears and the world doesn't fall around us, some of that fear falls away. The current reality clarifies itself in our mind. The conversation really matters in these moments. Coaching is an excellent tool for overcoming and managing fear in the short term.

But don't project coaching as a tool for long term fear management. If your concerns are taking up a significant portion of your day every day, that's not a coaching issue. It's probably time for one of those everyday counseling conversations with an appropriate professional.

A bit of fear will also identify the things that we value the most. One of the coaches in our network LOVES coaching clients when they can name something of which they are afraid. He's realized that we often fear losing an accomplishment we've made or not getting where we want to go, and that fear is powerful motivation for us.

What if using coaching hacks means we take it even one step further? A former colleague of mine in the broadcasting business used to say. **If it's not a little scary, it might not be worth doing.** Even a little bit of fear can indicate that you're taking on something that will end up being significant and meaningful for you. Fear can be a helpful trigger that leads to accomplishment. Leverage that for all it's worth!

The Key Habit: Help you client name the fear they're feeling, no matter how big or small.

What Now/Next: It becomes much easier to help someone else speak to their fear if we are in touch with our fears. Make a list of the things that scare you, ranging from being deathly afraid to things that startle you. Which one(s) are most likely to give you motivation?

Hack: Marry a repeatable conversation map AND a plan for the full arc of the coaching relationship!

The idea is to use a basic, repeatable pattern in both your coaching conversations (micro) and your coaching relationships (macro) so that you deliver a consistent experience to your client.

Master the fundamentals of coaching, so you're prepared to coach in every situation.

You may vary from this from time-to-time, but this is a foundational approach to diving into coaching.

Every coaching relationship has seasons. Spring and summer are excellent. But some coaching relationships have a particular winter and a definite fall.

Be prepared for the seasons to change. Intake process

Here's what the basic coaching conversation looks like: Follow the CHAIN. We've spent a lot of time on this in this book. The CHAIN is a great coaching hack.

That's the micro.

The Macro looks at the overall seasons of the coaching conversations.

Intake: Finding out what you need to know about the person you might be coaching. Determining if you can develop enough relationship to ask hard questions. Identify a purpose for the coaching relationship. Develop an agreement between coach and client.

Clarity: This is a season for confirming why the relationship exists. You'll dig beneath the surface and confirm what is going on in the relationship.

Vision: This is all about getting clear on where the relationship is going and the tension between where the client is now and where they want to end up. The pressure is powerful.

Implement: This season is about making a plan and executing a plan. This plan should be in writing.

Celebrate: What went right? What didn't? What can you celebrate?

On the upside, you develop relationship with the client. On the downside, you are moving away from managing the relationship to providing accountability, so the client begins to implement actions and plans that THEY choose.

There is one other piece to all this that will help you customize your coaching: there should be a developmental model that predicts how your client will change over the lifetime of the coaching relationship. Coaches super-serve their clients here. It's also where your experience makes a big difference in who you coach and how you coach them.

The Key Habit: Having an understanding of both how an individual conversation will go AND how the full relationship will play out will make you more productive.

What Now/Next: What repeatable conversation map do you use? What will you do to develop the arc of the coaching relationship with your client?

Hack: Coaching is a muscle. Use it to get stronger.

The gym is not my friend. Working out would be near the bottom of my list of things I want to do.

But I'm always happy when finished. Usually, I feel great. And I like the results: more energy, better muscle tone, the fact that I can eat more of what I want to eat. The positives outweigh the negatives, but I have this mental block.

I just don't want to go.

My brain just can't see why I would want to pick up heavy things, just to put them down. And then pick that same massive thing up AGAIN.

The day after the gym is even worse! My first few steps out of bed on the day after a workout are AGONY. Rationalizing "no pain, no gain" will only take you so far.

The struggle is real.

Weightlifting does make you stronger. The fibers in your muscles get broken down, and when they repair themselves, they come back stronger. And larger. Human beings prefer bigger muscles to smaller ones. The natural order of things draws us to people who are more fit.

Everyone knows someone who exercises regularly. Most of us have thought "*I wish I were in shape* like so-and-so." Putting in the time in the gym makes a difference: energy, vitality, a longer life, the list goes on.

You have to use what you've got to get better. When you use coaching hacks, it's the same way. Practice makes it easier and produces benefits that would be hard to acquire any other way.

Coaching is a muscle. Use that muscle if you want to get stronger. Even our brains work this way. The axons and dendrites in our gray matter get more closely connected every time we do something new. The first time we try something, there's only a single connection, and only a trickle of neurological information passes. Each time we repeat a task more brain areas connect. That's why doing something the first time is so much harder than doing it the thousandth time.

With every repetition, the neurological pipe grows. Tasks get easier. As with anything you want to be good at doing, you have to practice.

Don't just read this book, go out and do something with it what you've read. Be generous with someone. Listen first, then ask the best questions you can. Think of it as a lather, rinse, repeat cycle that makes your conversations more useful.

The Key Habit: Get coaching! Use what you've learned!

What Now/Next: When is the next conversation when you can use what you've read? What about the one after that? Try to implement one coaching hack in every conversation.

**Section 4: I've Read the Book.
Now, What Do I Do?**

Using Coaching Hacks Every Day

When you use coaching hacks, your conversations change. You become more attuned to what is important for the other person. You help the people around you make decisions. You challenge them to swing into action and get stuff done. You even help others to reflect on what they've accomplished and what they've learned from their progress.

You've heard it before: coaching changes everything.

But you know what? Coaching hacks can change *just about* everything. You just have to use them. Remind yourself that every conversation is a chance to discover insight that leads to application. It just takes the right orientation and a little preparation.

Get yourself into a coaching mindset by flipping back through this book and asking "What am I reading that makes me excited?" Or "Who would respond well to these coaching hacks?" You might even want to check in with yourself by asking things like "What scares me about this?" or "What's behind the tension I'm feeling right now?"

Pick out 4 or 5 of the hacks you've read and include them in your conversations. Test which Hacks work for you. Pay attention to the things that come out of your mouth naturally and which ones don't. And monitor where you have an impact on the people around you.

That's using coaching hacks to develop the people around you!

If you're wondering how other people are using Coaching Hacks, please follow the hashtag #coachinghacks on Twitter, Facebook and Instagram. You'll find plenty of inspiration there!

Should I become a coach?

Moment of full transparency here, an author's Articulate Moment: I hope you're saying "*Jonathan, what IREALLY want to do is to become a coach.*"

Nailing the coaching hacks will not make you a coach. It will start you on the path, but becoming a coach takes work. Every good coach I know has integrated coaching hacks into their life and coaching.

Becoming a coach takes three things: training, experience and ability to evaluate how you're doing. The combination approach equips you with new skills, gives you chances to practice, and teaches you to understand when you're clicking on all cylinders.

If you've caught the coaching bug, using coaching hacks will get you started. But you can't develop the kind of professional coaching skills that you'll need to earn a credential just by reading this book.

Go out there and coach. And get to training. Read the next section if you're thinking about training. It will help you decide what to do next.

If you want to learn to evaluate how you're doing, coaching experience and training will help. But you also need the ability to check in with yourself and immediately assess your skills and your results. Maybe it would be helpful to hear what I do when I coach.

My evaluation happens in two phases, right after the session and about a month later.

Immediately after the session, I ask some fundamental questions:
- How is my client feeling?
- What did my client get that they said they wanted?
- How much progress did we make toward the client's goals?
- How did I do in comparison to the ICF core coaching competencies?

A few weeks later, I revisit the session...On tape.

In CoachNet's Integrated Coach Training, recorded coaching sessions are a tool to objectively evaluate what students are doing well--and where they can improve.

Listening to a recording of your voice can be painful. No one--I mean, NO ONE--thinks they sound like on tape. (Our voices sound differently in our heads because we hear ourselves mostly through the tissue in our heads rather than our ears.)

But over the last 15 years, the majority of the real growth I've had as a coach has come from listening back to my sessions after they occurred.

Here are 13 things I've learned from listening to recordings of my coaching sessions:

1. **I don't connect with people as smoothly as I'd like.** The most glaring change I have made in my coaching is to listen to how my clients are doing in the first few minutes of each session. I tend to gloss over what they're saying and to miss vital information about where they are. My agenda for the session often takes over!

2. **My questions don't always include context.** General, open-ended questions are the lifeblood of coaching, but without some real context, they are not as powerful as I want them to be. Real breakthrough only comes with the background.

3. **The best question is personal.** Aim to ask questions that only the person you're talking with can answer. If the same question works with multiple clients, re-think what you're saying!

4. **Silence is my friend, and it never lasts as long as I feel it does.** Three to five seconds of silence NEVER seems out of place in a coaching conversation...even when I'm DYING for a client to fill it. That quiet time is a gift, and I snatch the gift away when I jump in too soon.

5. **The client's tone and pace in conversation speaks volumes.** When they pause or think for a moment, or stumble over a few words, there's a reason. A significant portion of the breakthroughs my clients have come when I ask about a change in tone or an extra few seconds of silence. The client will tell you when they have a new insight; you just have to listen.

6. **Coaching facilitates new learning better than any other approach.** Every good coach helps their clients get stuff done. Excellent coaches draw new self-knowledge or insight out of their clients. That kind of wisdom only comes from follow up questions or observation.

7. **Consulting is easy, but usually not helpful.** My advice or input flows much too easily. Coaches draw out...of the CLIENT. Learn to resist the urge to push

something into the conversation. And when you're drawing out, BE QUIET. Let the client talk through what they're thinking and feeling.

8. **The relationship is everything.** When a client trusts their coach, you have permission to ask the hard question. The hard question is what separates you from every other relationship the client has.

9. **My language doesn't matter.** When I get too caught up in what I'm saying or how I'm saying it, understanding and clarity fall away. I commit to using the client's language because of my recordings. Tailor your conversation to each client.

10. **Letting a little time pass before listening helps me be more objective.** If I remember for sure what I said in a session, the recording loses value. Being surprised by what I hear helps me evaluate the quality.

11. **When I'm coaching well, I don't say much.** The client has complete control of the agenda for the conversation, and I'm there to partner with them so that they can get where they want to go. A good rule of thumb is 80% of the time the client is speaking, and I only yak 20% or less.

12. **Humor is only helpful when it draws coach and client closer.** A joke helps to diffuse tension and makes the relationship authentic. BUT without a real sense of when and how much, it's easy to distract the client from what they're there to address.

13. **You don't need to record every session.** A good evaluation habit records each client once or twice over the life of a relationship. My preference is to review one session early in a relationship and one near the end of each engagement. The comparison shows how willing I am to serve each client on their terms and not mine.

Do you still want to be a coach? I'd encourage you. There's nothing better! It's the fast track to developing the people around you!

Bonus Hack: Training is for the coach. Credentials are for the client.

Over the last 20 years, I've led hundreds of hours of coach training and worked with thousands of coaches in dozens of events. Some events have been online, others have been in large conference rooms or hotel meeting rooms, and still others have been in churches or not-for-profit organizations.

Two types of potential coaches show up: the ones who want to master the skill of coaching and the people who want the satisfaction of earning a coaching credential.

Learning the skill set for coaching is not the same as earning a credential. Some great coaches do not have a professional credential. And some credential holders are, shall we say, not skilled coaches. Ideally, a coach would demonstrate mastery AND earn a credential, but that's just not the case in every situation.

In reality, coaches are not trained. Coaches develop. It takes time. And effort. And coaching in training is different than coaching in the wild.

Here's a rule by which to run your coaching practice: Your experience gets you hired. The client's experience gets you rehired. Another way to put it is that **training is for the coach. Credentials are for the client.**

It all comes down to what you can do. Your credential will catch client's attention. Earn a credential. The process will make you better. But what you can do as a coach is much more dependent on the kind of coaching skills you have and how satisfied your clients are.

Gain experience, and get into training. Evaluate your coaching intentionally. Earn a credential if you want one. But be sure to develop your skills. You'll be glad you did.

The Key Habit: Sharpen your coaching skills with every relationship.

What Now/Next: Find a solid training program, like CoachNet. And surround yourself with quality coaches who will help you develop.

Integrated Coach Training Options

The CoachNet Training Team has put together a process that will help you maximize your coach development. Integrated Coach Training follows a repeatable framework:

Thinking >> Skills >> Integrate >> Habits

Figure 9 -- How You Can Make Coaching a Part of Your Life

Integrated Coach Training begins with introducing the mental model for coaching to potential coaches. Solid mental models make learning the skills for coaching a quick and easy process.

As you repeat your new ways of thinking and apply your new skills, you discover the unique voice and posture that helps coaching integrate seamlessly into your everyday life and conversations, both at home and at work. The last phase is developing habits that support your coaching skills as they become a core part of who you are.

Integrated Coach Training is over 170 hours of course work, and can be customized to help you become the kind of coach you feel called to be! Our graduates have become executive coaches, life coaches, leadership coaches, startup coaches, ministry coaches, and some others! What do you think you might want to do in coaching?

Integrated Coach Training is offered entirely online, and builds out four distinct kinds of classes:
- Anchor Courses: 20 hours with a mix of instruction, discussion/processing, and live practice coaching with your classroom.

- Lab Courses: 8 hours live coaching practice with immediate feedback from the instructor.
- Assessment Courses: 4-hour courses split equally between self-assessment and group processing conversations.
- Elective Courses: 4-hour courses focusing on specialized coaching skills or improving your coaching process and system.

CoachNet has trained over 5,000 coaches since 1999, and we've helped coaches earn every credential in the ICF family.

Want to know more about Integrated Coach Training from CoachNet? Visit our website at http://www.coachnet.org/training.

If you use Coaching Hacks, you'll be pleasantly surprised at how much impact your conversations can have!

If you are a coach, these simple ideas can hone your impact. Your clients will leave every conversation celebrating that the lightbulb went off. Accept the charge of helping people articulate what's most important to them. Use *Coaching Hacks* to help with this challenge!

But there's one final thought I want to leave with you: It's a great privilege to be in a coaching-style relationship with another person, but always remember that every close relationship we have changes both parties a little bit. You've probably heard the thing about how we become like the five people with whom we spend the most time. That's because we leave a little bit of ourselves in relationship, and pick up a little bit of who they are.

In a recent training, this idea sunk in for one of the students. You could almost see the light bulb turn on over the other person's head.

The group had been working on listening skills, and one student was trying out their new skills on me. He fed back a summary of what I was saying to them. It was something like *"What I think you're saying is that one of the prime jobs of a coach is to encourage the person you're coaching."*

Yep. The group was listening, not just hearing. The lightbulb was on. The look on this coach-in-training's face, however, told me that this realization was troubling.

"But what if the coach is feeling discouraged...even about their coaching? What do I—err, a coach—do then?"

Mirroring a client's comments/posture/behavior is a powerful way to build relationship or develop direct communication. That same mirroring--intentional or not--can also share less-than-positive outcomes and mindsets between coach and client.

A coach's behavior/posture is contagious. Good things flow when the coach is in a positive, upbeat place. But when life gets the better of a coach, what do you do?

Every coach bumps up against this at some point. You know the client needs an encouraging word or question, and there's just nothing in the tank for you to offer.

Usually, a lack of good self-care or healthy boundaries causes what I call *Empty Tank Syndrome.* Any coach has several strategies available to manage the disconnect between the difference in your levels of optimism or encouragement.

Reflect on what is causing your discouragement. Sometimes just admitting what has gotten you down takes care of it. And some deeper thinking can often help you discover areas of your coaching that need attention.

Talk to YOUR coach. Coaches are encouragers, and that is one of the main things a client receives from their coach. You should be tapping into this source as well. *Every coach should HAVE a coach!*

Evaluate your calendar. Personally, the most common source of discouragement for me is when I have too much going on and not enough space between commitments. One of the most encouraging moments I face is when I wrap up and remove projects from my calendar/To Do list. The freedom that comes with that clean-up is exhilarating!

Pray. Coaching is a calling. Getting in touch (or back in touch) with the source of that calling is like taking a drink of cold water on a hot day.

Get some continuing education. Often discouragement comes when a coach feels like their skills have fallen into a rut. Attend a training event or coach's gathering to add new energy to your practice.

Exercise. If I'm honest about it, this is the one I do the least...And it's probably the one that makes the most difference. Your mood can change dramatically with just 10-20 minutes of movement. And that is contagious.

Engage the practice of gratitude. For most Americans in general and most coaches in particular, there are many more reasons to be thankful than to focus on where we're left wanting or missing something else. Investing in a practice of gratitude can help you focus on what you have and not what you're missing.

It's much easier just to keep going than to stop and take care of yourself. But remember that whether you use coaching hacks or are a full-time professional coach, you're not just taking care of yourself, you're also taking care of your clients.

The Ultimate Way to Hack Your Life

So, which of the Coaching Hacks hits closest to home for you? Which one(s) can you see yourself using? Which ones are a struggle to imagine coming out of your mouth?

Remember the power of what you have here: coaching changes everything. Once you help another person to say it, they have taken a step to doing it. That matters.

When you use coaching hacks, you become more generous. It's no longer about you. It's about the other person, or sometimes about us together. That matters.

There's too much me and not enough us in the world. When you use coaching hacks, you take a step to remedying this imbalance. That matters.

Coaching changes everything. THAT matters.

I'd love to hear your feedback. Shoot me an email sometime. I'd love to hear stories about how you use coaching hacks to make your conversations more useful. Send me the good, the bad, the ugly and the hilarious. Any story is welcome. My email is jonathan@jonathanreitz.com.

But even if you don't reach out to me, definitely try to use coaching hacks. Coaching hacks work. It's the very nature of a hack…a simple trick to make it easier to get something done. They're simple, and I believe they will make you more effective. Especially if you want to develop the people around you.

And that's the ultimate measure of making a conversation more effective. And a pretty good way to hack your way through life. Coaching changes everything.

Acknowledgements

Authors often talk about their books like parents talk about their children. If it takes a village to raise a child, books come from a similar set of relationships and influences. *Coaching Hacks* would not have been possible without the encouragement of three people.

Mark LeBlanc is my small business coach. He has focused me on what I do best and helped grow CoachNet into an unique training entity. Thank you.

Editing for this book was done by Lindsey Ivory. Thanks Lindsey! You made me sound better than I ever thought I would! I appreciate the great work.

Judy Pence heard all the Coaching Hacks first hand as they popped into my head over the years. Thanks for listening. And thanks for pushing me to write them down.

Appendix:
Helpful Tools for Coaches

Best Practices in Coaching

My friend Jeff Harrison is the principal of my daughter's high school. He often says that "Parents don't prepare the path for their kids. Parents prepare their kids for the path." These best practices are like that. They're not going to prepare you for every situation, but they will be a good set of guidelines for making the most of coaching situations.

The links in each section will take you to a part of this book that explores the topic further.

Prep for a coaching session. Have a game plan. Maybe it's only knowing the first question you're going to ask, but don't walk in cold. See Coaching starts BEFORE the conversation.

Develop a solid coaching agreement so time is used efficiently. See The client ALWAYS gets to choose.
Look for:
- The general topic for the conversation
- A specific outcome for the conversation
- What the other person wants to take away

Limited closed ended questions. And make your questions short and personal when you can.
- Closed >> Open >> Contextual >> Personal
  See The potential power of a question is inversely proportional to its length.

Coach asks permission to move in a new direction.
- Coach asks permission to offer input.
- Then follows with open ended question for application.
  See Ask in. Question out.

Questions probe beneath the surface.
- Work on root causes and not symptoms.
- Be the Arsonist when appropriate and the fireman when it's an emergency
  See Focus on root causes, not presenting symptoms.

Be generous all the time.
- Coach takes on client language, not the other way around.

- Coach is economical in use of all language and word choice. Don't belabor the point.
  See <u>Being generous wins.</u>

Draw out both plans (long term) and actions (short term).
- It's about both what the client will do now (before the next conversation), and
- What they will get done over the life of your work together.
- Plan your work. Work your plan.
  See <u>Implement: Getting into action.</u>

Seek out training and work with a mentor coach. You'll be surprised how much difference that makes.
- Every coach should also have a coach.

The Chain Model: A Simple Roadmap to Repeatable, Linked Conversations

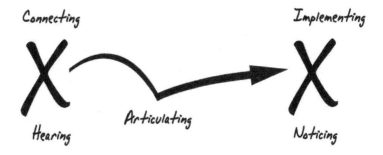

Figure10 -- The CHAIN Model. Use it. You'll like it.

You can use this simple coaching guide to work with a client in a single conversation on almost any issue. Be sure to spend a few minutes in each of the five areas. Remember: in the most effective coaching conversations, the client talks 80% of the time!

Connecting
Measurements
- Establish/re-establish enough relationship/rapport to make coaching possible.
- Default to a generous, client-centric focus.
- Commit/Recommit to the purpose of the coaching relationship.
- Identify the client's starting point for the conversation/relationship. Connect and celebrate progress.
- Ask for/confirm opt in.

Key Questions for Connecting:
- What is going on for you right now?
- What has you really excited right now?
- What is weighing on you most heavily now?
- What do you want to talk about in this session?
- What, specifically, do you want to accomplish in this session?

Hearing
Measurements
- Listen for facts, emotions, motivations and the story underneath the story.
- Ask bold questions that help the client discover new insight.
- Dance a conversational dance with the client, centering on the client's agenda.
- Actively and accurately confirm what the client is saying, listening between the words if necessary.
- Establish and confirm the coaching agreement for the session/relationship.

Key Questions for Hearing:
- What is most important to you about your life/work/ministry?
- What do you really wish was different in your life/work/ministry?
- What are you learning about yourself as a result?
- What 1 or 2 issues are at the root of the subject of this session?
- What key issue(s) are causing this issue?

Articulating
Measurements
- Draw out new realizations and insights using the client's language.
- Patiently help the client frame and reframe what they want.
- Facilitate client brainstorming.
- While dancing between generous listening and bold questions, help the client name what their deepest needs (The Articulate Moment).
- Conduct the conversation so that the client chooses their way forward.

Key Questions for Articulating:
- What would be the ideal outcome or resolution to this issue?
- What changes do you need to make?
- What personal strengths are you going to use to make this change?
- What excites/scares you about this change?
- What obstacles will get in your way?

Implementing

Measurements

- Finalize the choice of action step, building on client forward motion.
- Ensure the action plan moves the client toward big picture goals.
- Develop action steps.
- Explore accountability systems.
- Confirm the timeline.

Key Questions for Implementing:
- What plan do you need to make?
- What are you willing to commit to doing?
- What will you do to hold yourself accountable?
- What timeline will you commit to?
- How committed are you to this plan/change?

Noticing

Measurements

- Discover points of celebration.
- Mark progress from the beginning (of the session and the relationship).
- Help the client name the change (and the connected emotions) they are experiencing.
- Connect current conversation with next outcomes.
- Confirm next conversation.

Key Questions for Noticing:
- What progress have you made in this conversation?
- What emotions come up when you look at how far you've come?
- What adjustments do you need to make, based on your progress?
- What are you doing to tune out your negative self-talk?
- What have you learned in this conversation?
- What now/next?

The International Coach Federation's Core Coaching Competencies

The International Coach Federation has developed 11 Core Competencies that masterful coaches use to serve their clients.

Find more at this link:
https://coachfederation.org/credential/landing.cfm?ItemNumber=2206&navItemNumber=576

The competencies are grouped into families that roughly indicate where in the coaching conversation each competency takes root.

Competency Families
A. Setting the Foundation
1. Meeting Ethical Guidelines and Professional Standards
2. Establishing the Coaching Agreement

B. Co-creating the Relationship
3. Establishing Trust and Intimacy with the Client
4. Coaching Presence

C. Communicating Effectively
5. Active Listening
6. Powerful Questioning
7. Direct Communication

D. Facilitating Learning and Results
8. Creating Awareness
9. Designing Actions
10. Planning and Goal Setting
11. Managing Progress and Accountability

Individual Competencies (with sub-behaviors)

A. Setting the Foundation

1. Meeting Ethical Guidelines and Professional Standards—Understanding of coaching ethics and standards and ability to apply them appropriately in all coaching situations.

1. Understands and exhibits in own behaviors the ICF Code of Ethics (see Code, Part III of ICF Code of Ethics).
2. Understands and follows all ICF Ethical Guidelines (see list).
3. Clearly communicates the distinctions between coaching, consulting, psychotherapy and other support professions.
4. Refers client to another support professional as needed, knowing when this is needed and the available resources.

2. Establishing the Coaching Agreement—Ability to understand what is required in the specific coaching interaction and to come to agreement with the prospective and new client about the coaching process and relationship.

1. Understands and effectively discusses with the client the guidelines and specific parameters of the coaching relationship (e.g., logistics, fees, scheduling, inclusion of others if appropriate).
2. Reaches agreement about what is appropriate in the relationship and what is not, what is and is not being offered, and about the client's and coach's responsibilities.
3. Determines whether there is an effective match between his/her coaching method and the needs of the prospective client.

B. Co-Creating the Relationship

3. Establishing Trust and Intimacy with the Client—Ability to create a safe, supportive environment that produces ongoing mutual respect and trust.

1. Shows genuine concern for the client's welfare and future.
2. Continuously demonstrates personal integrity, honesty and sincerity.
3. Establishes clear agreements and keeps promises.
4. Demonstrates respect for client's perceptions, learning style, personal being.
5. Provides ongoing support for and champions new behaviors and actions, including those involving risk-taking and fear of failure.
6. Asks permission to coach client in sensitive, new areas.

4. Coaching Presence—Ability to be fully conscious and create spontaneous relationship with the client, employing a style that is open, flexible and confident.

1. Is present and flexible during the coaching process, dancing in the moment.
2. Accesses own intuition and trusts one's inner knowing—"goes with the gut."
3. Is open to not knowing and takes risks.
4. Sees many ways to work with the client and chooses in the moment what is most effective.
5. Uses humor effectively to create lightness and energy.
6. Confidently shifts perspectives and experiments with new possibilities for own action.
7. Demonstrates confidence in working with strong emotions and can self-manage and not be overpowered or enmeshed by client's emotions.

C. Communicating Effectively

5. Active Listening—Ability to focus completely on what the client is saying and is not saying, to understand the meaning of what is said in the context of the client's desires, and to support client self-expression.

1. Attends to the client and the client's agenda and not to the coach's agenda for the client.
2. Hears the client's concerns, goals, values and beliefs about what is and is not possible.
3. Distinguishes between the words, the tone of voice, and the body language.
4. Summarizes, paraphrases, reiterates, and mirrors back what client has said to ensure clarity and understanding.
5. Encourages, accepts, explores and reinforces the client's expression of feelings, perceptions, concerns, beliefs, suggestions, etc.
6. Integrates and builds on client's ideas and suggestions.
7. "Bottom-lines" or understands the essence of the client's communication and helps the client get there rather than engaging in long, descriptive stories.
8. Allows the client to vent or "clear" the situation without judgment or attachment in order to move on to next steps.

6. Powerful Questioning—Ability to ask questions that reveal the information needed for maximum benefit to the coaching relationship and the client.

1. Asks questions that reflect active listening and an understanding of the client's perspective.
2. Asks questions that evoke discovery, insight, commitment or action (e.g., those that challenge the client's assumptions).
3. Asks open-ended questions that create greater clarity, possibility or new learning.
4. Asks questions that move the client toward what they desire, not questions that ask for the client to justify or look backward.

7. Direct Communication—Ability to communicate effectively during coaching sessions, and to use language that has the greatest positive impact on the client.

1. Is clear, articulate and direct in sharing and providing feedback.
2. Reframes and articulates to help the client understand from another perspective what he/she wants or is uncertain about.
3. Clearly states coaching objectives, meeting agenda, and purpose of techniques or exercises.
4. Uses language appropriate and respectful to the client (e.g., non-sexist, non-racist, non-technical, non-jargon).
5. Uses metaphor and analogy to help to illustrate a point or paint a verbal picture.

D. Facilitating Learning and Results

8. Creating Awareness—Ability to integrate and accurately evaluate multiple sources of information and to make interpretations that help the client to gain awareness and thereby achieve agreed-upon results.

1. Goes beyond what is said in assessing client's concerns, not getting hooked by the client's description.
2. Invokes inquiry for greater understanding, awareness, and clarity.
3. Identifies for the client his/her underlying concerns; typical and fixed ways of perceiving himself/herself and the world; differences between the facts and the interpretation; and disparities between thoughts, feelings, and action.
4. Helps clients to discover for themselves the new thoughts, beliefs, perceptions, emotions, moods, etc. that strengthen their ability to take action and achieve what is important to them.
5. Communicates broader perspectives to clients and inspires commitment to shift their viewpoints and find new possibilities for action.
6. Helps clients to see the different, interrelated factors that affect them and their behaviors (e.g., thoughts, emotions, body, and background).

7. Expresses insights to clients in ways that are useful and meaningful for the client.
8. Identifies major strengths vs. major areas for learning and growth, and what is most important to address during coaching.
9. Asks the client to distinguish between trivial and significant issues, situational vs. recurring behaviors, when detecting a separation between what is being stated and what is being done.

9. Designing Actions—Ability to create with the client opportunities for ongoing learning, during coaching and in work/life situations, and for taking new actions that will most effectively lead to agreed-upon coaching results.

1. Brainstorms and assists the client to define actions that will enable the client to demonstrate, practice, and deepen new learning.
2. Helps the client to focus on and systematically explore specific concerns and opportunities that are central to agreed-upon coaching goals.
3. Engages the client to explore alternative ideas and solutions, to evaluate options, and to make related decisions.
4. Promotes active experimentation and self-discovery, where the client applies what has been discussed and learned during sessions immediately afterward in his/her work or life setting.
5. Celebrates client successes and capabilities for future growth.
6. Challenges client's assumptions and perspectives to provoke new ideas and find new possibilities for action.
7. Advocates or brings forward points of view that are aligned with client goals and, without attachment, engages the client to consider them.
8. Helps the client "Do It Now" during the coaching session, providing immediate support.
9. Encourages stretches and challenges but also a comfortable pace of learning.

10. Planning and Goal Setting—Ability to develop and maintain an effective coaching plan with the client.

1. Consolidates collected information and establishes a coaching plan and development goals with the client that address concerns and major areas for learning and development.
2. Creates a plan with results that are attainable, measurable, specific, and have target dates.

3. Makes plan adjustments as warranted by the coaching process and by changes in the situation.
4. Helps the client identify and access different resources for learning (e.g., books, other professionals).
5. Identifies and targets early successes that are important to the client.

11. Managing Progress and Accountability—Ability to hold attention on what is important for the client, and to leave responsibility with the client to take action.

1. Clearly requests of the client actions that will move the client toward his/her stated goals.
2. Demonstrates follow-through by asking the client about those actions that the client committed to during the previous session(s).
3. Acknowledges the client for what they have done, not done, learned or become aware of since the previous coaching session(s).
4. Effectively prepares, organizes, and reviews with client information obtained during sessions.
5. Keeps the client on track between sessions by holding attention on the coaching plan and outcomes, agreed-upon courses of action, and topics for future session(s).
6. Focuses on the coaching plan but is also open to adjusting behaviors and actions based on the coaching process and shifts in direction during sessions.
7. Is able to move back and forth between the big picture of where the client is heading, setting a context for what is being discussed and where the client wishes to go.
8. Promotes client's self-discipline and holds the client accountable for what they say they are going to do, for the results of an intended action, or for a specific plan with related time frames.
9. Develops the client's ability to make decisions, address key concerns, and develop himself/herself (to get feedback, to determine priorities and set the pace of learning, to reflect on and learn from experiences).
10. Positively confronts the client with the fact that he/she did not take agreed-upon actions.

Endnotes

1. https://coachfederation.org/need/landing.cfm?ItemNumber=978&navItemNumber=567, under the first question "What is professional coaching?"

2 http://www.ahaprocess.com/relationships-make-all-the-difference/

3. *https://en.wikipedia.org/wiki/Pareto_principle*

4.
https://coachfederation.org/credential/landing.cfm?ItemNumber=2206&navItemNumber=576

5. F. Scott Fitzgerald. BrainyQuote.com, Xplore Inc, 2017. https://www.brainyquote.com/quotes/quotes/f/fscottfit100572.html, accessed June 19, 2017.

6" https://www.brainyquote.com/quotes/quotes/m/michelange386296.html

7. https://www.brainyquote.com/quotes/quotes/c/charlesrs388332.html